Penal Substitution
ON TRIAL

How Does the Death and
Life of Jesus Save Us?

Philip Hess

Unless otherwise noted, Scriptures are taken from the New King James Version®. Copyright © 1982 by Thomas Nelson. Used by permission. All rights reserved.

Scriptures quotations marked NASB are taken from the New American Standard Bible® (NASB), Copyright © 1960, 1962, 1963, 1968, 1971, 1972, 1973, 1975, 1977, 1995 by The Lockman Foundation Used by permission. www.Lockman.org

Scriptures marked NRSV are from the New Revised Standard Version Bible, copyright 1989, Division of Christian Education of the National Council of the Churches of Christ in the United States of America. Used by permission. All rights reserved.

© 2020 Philip Hess

This work is licensed under the Creative Commons Attribution-NonCommercial-NoDerivatives 4.0 International License. To view a copy of this license, visit http://creativecommons.org/licenses/by-nc-nd/4.0/ or send a letter to Creative Commons, PO Box 1866, Mountain View, CA 94042, USA

With proper attribution and per the terms of the license above, this book may be quoted from or copied for distribution free of charge as long as it is not sold or altered in any way.

Cover design: Justin Ebersole
Interior and text design: Glenn Martin

This is my Father's world,

The battle is not done,

Jesus who died shall be satisfied

And earth and Heav'n be one!

- Maltie D. Babcock

To Daddy and Mother

who taught me about God's love and salvation.

TABLE OF CONTENTS

Preface	vii
Acknowledgements	xi

Part 1: Penal Substitution Examined

1.	Too Familiar to Be False?	1
2.	Penal Substitution	7
3.	Problems with Penal Substitution	21
4.	Imputed Righteousness	41
5.	Faith	55
6.	Atonement Theology in History	63

Part 2: Penal Substitution Replaced

7.	Making Sense Out of This Mess	75
8.	Why Did We Need Some Good News?	79
9.	The Good News Arrives	87
10.	Christ the Victor	95
11.	Further Thoughts About the Atonement	121
12.	Life!	133
	Conclusion	139

Addendum: A Word About Wrath and Righteous Judgment	145
Appendix A. Words About Words	149
Appendix B. Penal Substitution Proof Texts Examined	169
Appendix C. List of New Testament Atonement Verses	185
Bibliography	219

PREFACE

I have two burdens that have inspired this writing. The first is that we appreciate and magnify the character of God. Some theological beliefs that are held today have tended to distort people's views of God, damaging his reputation and obscuring his glory. The particular theological view that I am concerned with here is called "The Penal Substitution Model of the Atonement," or "Penal Substitutionary Atonement" (PSA). The Penal Substitution Model of the Atonement is an explanation of how Jesus' death on the cross brought us salvation. It relies on certain suppositions about how justice works, how sin is remitted, and the character of God.

The second burden is related. Within large sectors of Christianity, there are unbiblical ideas taught and defended that have done great damage to the faith of Jesus Christ. Among these are the doctrines of cheap grace[1] and unconditional eternal security. Certain teachings of Calvinism, and the common Protestant understanding of imputed righteousness, while not in themselves deadly, have also tended to lead people astray. These teachings all have something in

---

[1] This is what Dietrich Bonhoeffer called it. Proponents of this view often refer to it as "Free Grace." In his book, *The Cost of Discipleship,* Bonhoeffer criticized the views of those who promote "Free Grace" saying, "*Cheap grace is the preaching of forgiveness without requiring repentance, baptism without church discipline, Communion without confession . . . Cheap grace is grace without discipleship, grace without the cross, grace without Jesus Christ, living and incarnate.*"

common: they all rest on a particular foundation. Many have exposed these teachings as unbiblical, but they have remained. Why? It is my conviction that what is needed is the removal of the foundation upon which these teachings rest. This foundation is "The Penal Substitution Model of the Atonement."

When I first heard the Atonement explained from a perspective of "Christus Victor", I found the message to be revolutionary. It gave me a greater appreciation for the work of Christ on the cross, and a deeper thanks for what he had done for me. It also began to answer a question I had been wrestling with.

In sharing the gospel with people, I felt a certain tension. When we tell them that salvation is by faith, do we quickly follow up by teaching the necessity of obedience? Won't that just make them trust in their works? Yet I feared that unless I quickly followed up "Believe on the Lord Jesus Christ and be saved" with teaching about how to live, they would think that if they would just believe, obedience and lifestyle would not matter.

I came to see that part of the problem was an inadequate presentation of the gospel. Many of us have been taught to present the gospel in a way that focuses on man's problem with God, and on how God "took his punishment," "freed him from guilt," and "let him off the hook."

When I began to grasp a bit more of the breadth and depth of the Atonement, I saw that a "Christus Victor" view leads to a thoroughly biblical gospel message. This gospel emphasizes that Jesus is the King, that he has showed up and defeated Satan, that he has offered deliverance to the captives—and that what you must do is repent and follow him to share in his life, in his kingdom, and in his destiny. This message makes the transition from believing on Jesus to living as a citizen of his kingdom quite natural. It does not set up a dichotomy between believing and obeying.

As I studied the Atonement, a third burden developed. I became increasingly convinced that Penal Substitution is at odds with the teaching of the original Christian faith about following Jesus, especially as described in the Sermon on the Mount. If Jesus really came to reveal God to us, and teach us to be like him in character, then Jesus' life and teachings describe what that means. If, however, God's character requires that he cannot forgive sin without justice being satisfied (and hence must pour out his wrath on Jesus), then he calls us in the gospels to be different in character from his own character. The historic Christian teaching about suffering love does not harmonize well with this picture of God. Thus, as Christians from the historic peace churches accept and promote Penal Substitution and related ideas, they gradually assimilate into mainstream Protestantism.

Penal Substitution has caused a split between salvation and ethics, a split that is absent in the Gospels. On the day of judgment when Jesus says to some,

> 'Depart from Me . . . for I was hungry and you gave Me no food; I was thirsty and you gave Me no drink',[1]

he shows no hint of a divide between salvation and ethics, or "faith and works"[2]. How does this square with "For by grace you have been saved through faith . . . not of works, lest anyone should boast"?[3]

The reason that Penal Substitution divorces salvation from ethics is because it is *reductionistic*. It tends to reduce man's problem to a pending punishment, and then offers an incorrect solution in which Jesus takes that punishment instead. Many

---

[1] Matthew 25:41-42
[2] James 2:14-26
[3] Ephesians 2:8, 9

who have seen problems with Penal Substitution have proposed equally reductionistic alternatives, such as the Moral Influence theory, René Girard's Scapegoat theory, and Waldron Scott's Intercessor model.

As I looked for books on the Atonement to be able to recommend to others, I encountered a problem. Few presented an understanding of God's atonement with a view that was solidly grounded in historic Christianity and Jesus' teachings in the Gospels. And many books on Atonement theology were written by theologians to theologians. They were often boring and difficult. Thus, in this book, I have tried to put more detailed discussions in the appendices.

For those who must know ahead of time, my approach to understanding the Atonement will be broadly "Christus Victor". However, we will focus less on Christ's defeat of Satan and more on our need for deliverance from sin and death. We will attempt to understand how Christ's death brought us life. Elements of "recapitulation" and "moral influence" will be expressed.

My goal in this book has been to set forth a robust criticism of Penal Substitution, and to supplant it with a robust, biblical understanding of the Atonement. My hope is that we will glorify God by rejoicing in his character and grace. It is my desire that we grow in understanding together and develop a deeper appreciation for God, his purpose for the cosmos, and his gracious gift to us.

Philip Hess

ACKNOWLEDGEMENTS

Were it not for the inspiration and help of many others, this book would never have been completed. A special thanks to Mike Atnip for feedback, critique, and insights, and to Glenn Martin for editing, discussion, and much help. Thank you to the numerous friends who have discussed the subject and bounced around ideas, read my work, pointed out problems, given editorial feedback, and in various ways encouraged me to keep going. And most of all, a special thanks to my wife Betsy, for bearing with me during this project and whose self-sacrifice of her own scintillating interests in deference to her husband's dry theological ones was the only way I was able to read and write.

PART 1

PENAL SUBSTITUTION EXAMINED

CHAPTER 1

TOO FAMILIAR TO BE FALSE?

If a statement is made often enough, people will believe it without thinking it through. This is what makes propaganda and brainwashing effective. Recently, I've been thinking about a quote:

> No one has the right to hear the gospel twice, while there remains someone who has not heard it once.[1]

The statement sounds so right and reasonable. But it is untrue for a couple of reasons: First, how could we prove that someone has a *right* to hear the gospel? The gospel is a *gift*. A gift, by definition, is something we don't get by right, but instead by someone's graciousness. But beyond that, is this how Jesus operated? Did he preach the gospel once to the twelve disciples and then say, "I'm not going to let you hear the gospel again until all the Chinese, Ethiopians, and Native Americans have heard it"?

Another example of this kind of untrue but widely believed statement is the axiom that America was supposedly founded

---

[1] Oswald J. Smith

on:

> We hold these truths to be self-evident, that all men . . . are endowed by their Creator with certain unalienable Rights, that among these are Life, Liberty, and the pursuit of Happiness.[1]

How are "life, liberty, and the pursuit of happiness" unalienable rights? When a baby is stillborn, did God take away its right to life? When God tolerated and regulated slavery in the Old Testament, was he violating someone's right to liberty?[2] When a husband leaves his wife and marries someone else, will not the first wife's "right to the pursuit of happiness" ring a little hollow? Perhaps it would be more accurate to tell her that she has a right to the pursuit of *holiness,* and that this will ultimately make her happy. The world is full of people who have pursued their own happiness and, in the process, violated others. We surely must concede that the blessings of "life, liberty, and the pursuit of happiness" are, like the "right" to hear the gospel, actually gifts from God. They cannot be strictly said to be "rights."

Before challenging another statement that you may have heard all your life, let me tell you a couple stories:[3]

---

[1] Jefferson, Thomas, "The Declaration of Independence", 1776

[2] I'm not saying that God wants an arrangement in which one man owns another. People who care about others and who follow the teachings of Jesus are always promoting the welfare of everyone, and this always involves speaking out against involuntary servitude. In the Jewish nation, a man might sell himself into temporary slavery, and God gave many laws to protect slaves from various abuses.

[3] These stories each highlight a singular aspect taught by Penal Substitution. They do not illustrate the full teaching of the theory, and should not be assumed to be comprehensively representing it. However, it is important to understand that this is how some hear the message of Penal Substitution, such as an atheist I quote in chapter two: "I think this whole vicarious salvation is stinking horrible. Let's take someone innocent and torture her to death because someone else did something horrible."

> There was once a righteous man who lived in a wicked city. Day by day, he walked about the city and saw its abominations. He saw men murder for money. He saw husbands beating their wives. He saw the rich oppress the poor. He saw little children molested. Day by day, his anger and hatred of all the wickedness and injustice grew. Finally, it came to the boiling point, and something had to be done. So, he brutally murdered his only son. Finally, he had a chance to expend his wrath on someone, and was able to release his anger.[1]

And a second story:

> Once there was a judge who had reason to be angry. A band of wicked men had molested his daughter. Now, they were brought to the bar, and he had a chance to throw the book at them—a chance for revenge—and to make them suffer for their crime! He brought the gavel down for a guilty verdict, but before they were hauled off to the whipping post, the judge's own son stepped forward. He said, "Dad, I know that you are just and will not be satisfied until someone is punished for this crime. I want to take these men's punishment." The judge was pleased by the character of his son. "You are right," he said. "A crime has been done. Justice will be satisfied as long as someone is punished for it." The son was hauled off to the whipping post, and justice was served.[2]

---

[1] Penal Substitution teaches that God's wrath had to be satisfied by coming down on someone, guilty or not. This story is solely intended to illustrate how very odd it would be to think that wrath could be satisfied by coming against an innocent party. This idea of the satisfaction of wrath can be heard in the popular song that says, "Till on that cross as Jesus died, The wrath of God was satisfied"; as well as in a quote from chapter two where R.C. Sproul says: "Here the fury of God raged against Him".

[2] This story illustrates justice being satisfied by an innocent party taking a punishment for the guilty party; is this not contrary to what we instinctively

I hope these stories seem ludicrous to you. We all know a little bit about justice and human feelings. No one feels justice has been done if an innocent person wants to take the punishment for someone who is guilty. No one finds that it is easier to forgive someone who has wronged us by taking out our wrath on someone else. That is not how forgiveness works. No one—except possibly very evil people—feels pleased if someone who is innocent is punished in the place of someone who is guilty. Yet that is what many have been attributing to God!

As I mentioned, here is another statement you may believe because you've heard similar things all your life. Does this statement sound reasonable to you?

> On the cross, Jesus endured the full weight of the wrath of God against sin. God punished him so that he could let us go free.

This statement has been made so often that few Christians challenge it. Instead, they just assume that it makes sense. I hope to show that this statement is not only inaccurate but also unreasonable.

We should really care about this because the character of God is at stake. The above statement about the satisfaction of God's wrath comes from what is known as the Penal Substitution Model of the Atonement. Many who see God as capricious or unreasonable find reinforcement for their feelings in this model. Many who look at God as an angry or inscrutable Father feel as they do because the natural tendencies of this model push them in that direction. Often, people get the idea that God the Father is the one who is wrathful and vengeful

---

know of justice? Does not this only make sense to those who have heard it so often as to not question how strange the notion is? In chapter two I quote atheist Michael Shermer: "God sacrificed himself to himself to save us from himself. This is barking mad!"

toward us, but Jesus is the one on our side who intervenes.[1,2]

---

[1] It is the popular level presentations that often sound especially bad. Careful presentations of Penal Substitution present a much fuller picture, and appeal to broader themes than only the satisfaction of justice. Some speak beautifully of God's love expressed in sending Jesus. Yet they all have a certain viewpoint of God's wrath and the satisfaction of his justice that does not properly display the character of God.

[2] It could be objected that Jesus is not some innocent bystander who happens to get victimized, because he himself is God. Therefore, it is not God punishing someone else instead of us, but God himself taking our punishment. However, while Penal Substitution claims that God himself bore our punishment and was the only one capable and qualified to do so, the question about how justice could thereby be satisfied remains unanswered.

Chapter 2

Penal Substitution

The Atonement, in theology, is the work of Jesus to save lost humanity and bring peace and unity between God and man. We know that Jesus died on the cross and rose from the grave. "Christ died for our sins, according to the Scriptures."[1] However, the Scriptures say many more things about *why* he died and *what* he accomplished. People try to fit these things together into atonement theories to explain what happened during these events and how it works to save us.

There are quite a number of different theories, or models. Among the more common or better-known ones are the Classic (Christus Victor) theory, the Ransom theory, the Recapitulation theory, the Satisfaction theory, the Moral Influence theory, and the Penal Substitution theory. Most common today among Protestants and Evangelicals is the Penal Substitution theory (also called Penal Substitutionary Atonement or PSA).

> Penal substitutionary atonement refers to the doctrine that Christ died on the cross as a substitute for sinners. God imputed the guilt of our sins to Christ, and he, in our place, bore the punishment that we deserve. This

---
[1] 1 Corinthians 15:3

was a full payment for sins, which satisfied both the wrath and the righteousness of God, so that He could forgive sinners without compromising His own holy standard.[1]

I would like to show that the Penal Substitution theory does not align with the Scriptures, that it is not the historic view of the church, and that it does not fit with our inherent understandings of right and justice. Further, much error and heresy either flows from or relies on this model of the Atonement. I would like to propose alternate ways of understanding the Atonement, steering the reader toward a more comprehensive understanding of Jesus' life and death from a different perspective.

The Penal Substitution model grew out of what is called the Satisfaction theory of the Atonement. The Satisfaction theory was first fully articulated in the eleventh century by a man named Anselm, a notable theologian and Archbishop of Canterbury. Later, another influential theologian and philosopher, Thomas Aquinas, refined the theory. A couple centuries later still, the Protestant reformers put the finishing touches on it. Today when many (especially Evangelicals and Protestants) think of the gospel, the only understanding they have is based upon the Penal Substitution model. Many are unaware that there are other ways of understanding the gospel message and the work of Christ.

Penal Substitution presented

As defended by its advocates, Penal Substitution states that man's problem is sin, and that he is therefore the enemy of a

---

[1] *Theopedia*, s.v. "Penal substitutionary atonement" accessed April, 2020 https://www.theopedia.com/penal-substitutionary-atonement

holy God. God cannot overlook sin; he cannot simply forgive it. Because God is just, he is obligated to bring punishment for sin or receive a satisfaction[1] for sin prior to extending forgiveness.

As the theory goes, because man was unable to pay the debt of punishment owed to God, God himself took the punishment due for our sin. He did this in the person of Jesus Christ, God the Son. To support this understanding, appeal is made to a number of Scripture passages. On the cross,[2] the full weight of God's wrath against sin came down on Jesus. This was possible because Jesus "Himself bore our sins in His own body on the tree."[3] When the wrath of God came down on Jesus, the demands of justice were thereby fulfilled and God was then free to forgive us without requiring us to be punished for our own sins. Because it was man who sinned, it had to be a man who took the punishment for sin. Hence Jesus needed to come as a man. But because Jesus is also God (and infinite), he was able to bear the punishment and atone for all sin, and he offers his infinite merit to us.

Many who hold these views would couple this idea with the doctrine of imputed righteousness. This states that our sins were imputed (i.e. transferred) to Jesus at his crucifixion, and that his merit (i.e. righteousness) is imputed to us. As God, his merit is infinite and so it can cover the sins of all who accept Christ as Savior.

Is it reasonable?

---

[1] Satisfaction is a legal term meaning "compensation for a loss or injury." In religious contexts, "reparation for sin that meets the demands of divine justice." *Webster's New Collegiate Dictionary,* 1977 s.v. "satisfaction."
[2] Some would add that Jesus also suffered the penalty for our sins in hell for the three days following his death.
[3] 1 Peter 2:24

If you're in the Protestant or Evangelical stream of influence, you may not have seen this presentation of Penal Substitution above as anything objectionable. The majority of Protestants and Evangelicals today accept this view as biblical; it is simply an article of faith in many Christian organizations that this is how the suffering and death of Jesus saves us. If you have had the gospel explained this way to you all your life, it may sound completely reasonable.

But to many non-Christians, this understanding of the gospel seems ludicrous. And, unfortunately, it is the only gospel they have heard. As one atheist put it to me:

> I think this whole vicarious salvation is stinking horrible! Let's take someone innocent and torture her to death because someone else did something horrible.

Or hear the viewpoint of atheist Michael Shermer, who in a recent debate titled, *Does God Exist*, commented, "God sacrificed himself, to himself, to save us from himself. This is barking mad!"[1]

Now, scoffers will scoff. The preaching of the cross will sound like foolishness to some. If Penal Substitution is biblical, by all means, let's defend it. On the other hand, if Penal Substitution is not taught in the Bible, and if there are better ways of understanding the Atonement, let's not set up unnecessary stumbling blocks in the way of unbelievers.[2]

---

[1] "'Does God Exist?' David Wood vs. Michael Shermer (Christian vs. Atheist Debate)," Acts17Apologetics, Published on October 30, 2016, YouTube video, at 47:10. https://www.youtube.com/watch?v=PMWKm40-dnM

[2] The foolishness of the cross message (1 Corinthians 1:18) is not intended to imply that it sounds illogical so much as that to those who don't see their need of salvation, the message will sound irrelevant or unnecessary.

Something missing?

You may have noticed that there was nothing in the presentation of Penal Substitution that touched on the teachings of Jesus. His miracles are not mentioned. His resurrection is not mentioned. As far as Penal Substitution is concerned, Jesus could have left the carpenter shop in Nazareth, walked into Jerusalem, gotten himself nailed to a cross, and stayed dead in the tomb. Yet our sins could still have been forgiven and we could have "gone to heaven," because—according to this view—the penalty would have been paid.

This highlights something about Western thought. We Westerners see the world through the framework of Roman law and its justice system focused primarily on retribution (retributive justice).[1] We tend to be more focused on sin as an individual problem than as a systemic, cosmic problem that needs to be dealt with. This tends to make us focus on our problem of guilt (culpability), and how to escape our pending punishment. Penal Substitution has a lot to say about cancellation of sins but little to say about undoing the effects of the curse, restoration of God's creation, defeat of Satan, and related themes.[2] So, it is no surprise that our view of salvation tends to be a very individualistic one: "I have a problem between me and God. God fixed it. Now I have a personal relationship with God."

---

[1] John Driver, *Understanding the Atonement for the Mission of the Church.* (Scottsdale, PA: Herald Press, 1986), 33.
[2] Josiah Trenham, in his book *Rock and Sand* says: "The great problem with Protestant teaching on salvation is its thorough-going reductionism. In the Holy Scripture and in the writings of the Holy Fathers salvation is a grand accomplishment with innumerable facets, a great and expansive deliverance of humanity from all its enemies: sin, condemnation, the wrath of God, the devil and his demons, the world, and ultimately death. In Protestant teaching and practice, salvation is essentially a deliverance from the wrath of God." Archpriest Josiah Trenham, *Rock and Sand: An Orthodox Appraisal of the Protestant Reformers and Their Teachings.* (Columbia, MO: Newrome Press LLC, 2018), 174.

Although Penal Substitution provides an answer for some of our concerns, it is less effective at answering the concerns of other worldviews.

> [A young Muslim man], after having numerous conversations with Evangelical Christians in America . . . declared, "You see things and explain them with legal terminology as if we are in a court. You talk so much about guilt and righteousness, of sin and its penalty, of condemnation and justification. I have been shown the Four Spiritual Laws, the Bridge Illustration, and Steps to Peace with God. They all follow logical syllogism and use legal terminology. But my paradigm, the lenses through which I look at reality, are not primarily those of guilt and righteousness. Mine are those of shame and honor, clean and unclean, fear and power. When I talk with American Christians, I feel like they are laying a guilt trip on me. Does your message have anything to say to me about my shame, my defilement, my fears?"[1]

The prior presentation of Penal Substitution gives us no help at all toward understanding why Jesus would say at the Last Supper, "I have finished the work which You have given Me to do."[2] Clearly, Jesus thought that he had already accomplished major things in the purpose of God prior to his crucifixion.

Faulty logic?

Not only does Penal Substitution not explain comprehensively much of what is emphasized in the gospel narratives, its own internal logic has some problems. Let me illustrate this by examining a modern-day articulation of Penal Substitution as

---

[1] Waldron Byron Scott, *What about the Cross: Exploring Models of the Atonement.* (Lincoln, NE: iUniverse, 2007), 81.
[2] John 17:4

found in a gospel tract. I know of nothing in the following quote that most of the Protestant reformers would have disagreed with:

> To make clear what an incredible thing He has done for you in the Gospel, let's look again to civil law: You are standing in front of a judge, guilty of *very* serious crimes. All the evidence has been presented and there is no doubt about your guilt. The fine for your crime is $250,000 or imprisonment, but you haven't two pennies to rub together. The judge is about to pass sentence... he lifts his gavel, when *someone you don't even know steps in and pays the fine for you.* The moment you accept that payment, you are free to go. Justice has been served, the law has been satisfied, and what's more, the stranger who paid your fine showed how much he cares for you. His payment was evidence of his love.
>
> That's what God did for you, in the person of Jesus Christ. You are guilty. He paid the fine 2,000 years ago. *It is that simple. . . .*
>
> His sacrificial death and resurrection mean that you no longer need to be in debt to the Law, and God can now grant you everlasting life if you obey Him – death no longer has a legal hold upon those who belong to Jesus Christ.[1]

The above quote seems to make sense because of a "bait and switch" technique. You are told that you are guilty of *very* serious crimes. Then, you are told that the penalty is a $250,000 fine. One problem with this analogy is that there are no very serious crimes that you can legally get out of by paying

---

[1] Ray Comfort. Excerpt from "Are You Good Enough to Go to Heaven?" (Bellflower, CA: Living Waters Publications)

money. When people are fined, it is because they have either done something relatively minor (like getting a parking ticket) or put someone in danger without actually hurting anyone (like going at a high speed through a construction zone). They are fined because the state is prosecuting and does not have an emotional investment in the case. The state is more concerned about money and efficiency rather than offended because you parked too long in one spot. In the example above, if our debt was really a financial one, it would make sense that someone else could step in and pay it off. However, when a person commits a very serious crime that emotionally affects someone else, the injured person would probably not be satisfied if someone tried to atone by paying them money. An offer of $250 *million* would likely be offensive to a loving parent whose child was murdered.[1] So to draw an accurate analogy, we would have to go back and imagine a scenario where we would be "satisfied" to have an innocent party punished to atone for the murder of our child. If we cannot imagine this satisfying our sense of justice, then how can we imagine that it would satisfy God's sense of justice?

I want to interject here that many who hold this view of the Atonement are sincere Christians, and I expect to see multitudes of them in heaven. While there are some essential beliefs that you must have to be a Christian, we are *not* saved by having all the correct theological beliefs. Rather, we continue saved because we continue to abide in the vine. So please understand that I'm not judging you or your Christian walk if you agree with the gospel presentation in the tract above. Yet the view presented in the tract leads to biblical and philosophical problems.

---

[1] I say this in the context of Western culture, which has had many of its values shaped by Christian influence. There may be cultures with a lower view of life that would not feel the same.

Leading to heresy?

Clearly, this view of salvation sees man's problem as primarily a legal one; and therefore, there must be a legal solution to the problem. The legal solution put forth by the Reformers is called "imputation".

Their teaching of imputation runs like this: At the cross, your sin, and that of all mankind, was *imputed to* (or put upon) Jesus. In response, God punished Jesus for man's sin that was upon him. Stated another way, God's wrath came down upon that sin in judgment. It is said that Jesus became the "lightning rod of God's wrath."[1]

Although you need to be righteous to be saved, you have no righteousness of your own. To remedy this, Jesus' righteousness, by a legal transfer, is credited (imputed) to your account. This is called double imputation: your sin to Jesus, his righteousness to you. This is explained to happen at the moment of conversion. When you accept that he bore your punishment, his righteousness is then credited to your account.

The first problem is that this is not found in Scripture; nowhere does Scripture state that Christ's righteousness is imputed to us. The second problem is that (in the minds of many), this removes any need for a Christian to be personally righteous. According to this view, Christ's righteousness covers you so that when God sees you, instead of seeing the vile filth that you really are, he instead sees Christ's righteousness covering you.

---

[1] A. W. Tozer says "The cross is the lightning rod of grace that short-circuits God's wrath to Christ so that only the light of His love remains for believers." Cited from A. W. Tozer, "Christian Quotes," oChristian, accessed April, 2019. http://christian-quotes.ochristian.com/Light-Quotes/page-4.shtml Another example is from Ethan Hansen, "My favorite verse," Mat-Su Valley Frontiersman, accessed May, 2020. https://www.frontiersman.com/my-favorite-bible-verse/article_b4d2fa08-b35b-11e7-9b7f-77ca0fa16040.html

This allows for the view that you do not need to be holy.[1]

Is imputing sin to Jesus an insult?

Martin Luther said:

> We are sinners and thieves, and therefore guilty of death and everlasting damnation. But Christ took all our sins upon him, and for them died upon the cross . . . all the prophets did foresee in spirit, that Christ should become the greatest transgressor, murderer, adulterer, thief, rebel, blasphemer, etc. that ever was . . . for he being made a sacrifice, for the sins of the whole world, is now an innocent person and without sins . . . our most merciful Father, seeing us to be oppressed, overwhelmed with the curse of the law, and so to be holden under the same that we could never be delivered from it by our own power, sent his only Son into the world and laid upon him all the sins of all men, saying: Be thou Peter that denier; Paul that persecutor, blasphemer and cruel oppressor; David that adulterer; that sinner which did eat the apple in Paradise; that thief which hanged upon the cross; and, briefly, be thou the person which hath committed the sins of all men; see therefore that thou pay and satisfy for them. Here now cometh the law and saith: I find him a sinner, and that such a one as hath taken upon him the sins of all men, and I see no sins but in him; therefore let him die upon the cross. And so he setteth upon him and killeth him. By this means the whole world is purged and cleansed from all sins, and so delivered from death and

---

[1] Many advocates of Penal Substitution do teach that Christians need to be holy. However, the view that you do not need to be personally holy logically flows from Penal Substitution and its corresponding ideas, and does not flow from some other views of the Atonement.

all evils.[1]

Adam Clarke, the Wesleyan commentator, called this

> ... a most blasphemous doctrine, *viz.*, that *our sins were imputed to Christ*, and that He was a *proper object of the indignation of divine justice,* because He *was blackened with imputed sin;* and some have proceeded so far as to say that *Christ may be considered the greatest of all sinners, because all of the sins of mankind,* or of *the elect* as they say, *were imputed to Him, and reckoned as His own.*[2]

A modern theologian, R. C. Sproul, stated,

> God the Father turned His back on the Son, cursing Him to the pit of hell while He hung on the cross. Here was the Son's 'descent into hell.' Here the fury of God raged against Him. His scream was the scream of the damned. For us.[3]

What are the consequences to God's honor if this statement is not true? If this is not what actually happened, the implications of making such statements are rather frightening. Job's friends claimed that God was punishing Job when in fact he was not, and God apparently found this offensive.

Other theological problems

---

[1] J.I. Packer, "Sola Fide: The Reformed Doctrine of Justification," Ligonier.org. Accessed April, 2020. https://www.ligonier.org/learn/articles/sola-fide-the-reformed-doctrine-of-justification/
[2] *Adam Clarke's Commentary on the Bible,* under "2 Corinthians 5:21".
[3] R.C. Sproul, "Treasuring Redemption's Price", Ligonier Ministries, accessed April, 2020. https://www.ligonier.org/learn/devotionals/treasuring-redemptions-price/

A whole set of problems of a more abstract theological nature flow from Penal Substitution due to the fact that it underpins the doctrines of Calvinism.

For the clearest example, consider the doctrine of "limited atonement". This doctrine states that Christ did not die for all sinners, but only the elect. The logic goes like this: if Christ bore the punishment for someone, then he or she *must necessarily* be saved. It would be unjust for Christ to be punished for someone's sins, but for them to also bear the punishment for their own sins in hell.[1],[2] (This is often referred to as double jeopardy.) Thus, if Christ died for all men, (according to this logic) all would be saved.

Calvinism[3], therefore teaches that Jesus only suffered and died for the elect—even though the Bible clearly teaches that Christ died for *all* men.[4] If, however, Christ's death was not even intended to pay the penalty for sins, the whole idea of limited atonement becomes irrelevant.

The doctrines of irresistible grace and perseverance of the elect are also linked to Penal Substitution. If Christ paid for

---

[1] For example, Calvinist James White says, "How will the opponent of a fully substitutionary and effective atonement respond to this argument? Does God the Father actually place the sins of those He knows will spend eternity in hell upon His Son?" (Dave Hunt and James White, *Debating Calvinism: Five Points, Two Views,* [Colorado Springs, CO: Multmonah Books, 2004], 173.)

[2] Another example is John Owen, in *The Death of Death in the Death of Christ,* Book 1, Chapter 3, where he uses Penal Substitution to argue limited atonement. He says, if "God imposed His wrath...and Christ underwent the pains of hell" for all men, why "are not all freed from the punishments of all their sins?"

[3] Some "Four Point Calvinists" believe in an "unlimited atonement". Of them, R. C. Sproul says: "I think that if a person really understands the other four points and is thinking at all clearly, he *must* believe in limited atonement because of what Martin Luther called a resistless logic. Still, there are people who live in a happy inconsistency. I believe it's possible for a person to believe four points without believing the fifth, although I don't think it's possible to do it consistently or logically." (R.C. Sproul, *The Truth of The Cross,* [Reformation Trust Publishing, 2007], 141-142.)

[4] John 3:16, 17, 1 Timothy 2:4

someone's sins, of course that person could not fail to receive the benefits that had been purchased for him, and of course he could not fall away. Augustus Toplady expressed the connection between Penal Substitution and perseverance of the elect this way:

> If Thou hast my discharge procured,
> And freely in my room endured
> The whole of wrath divine:
> Payment God cannot twice demand,
> First at my wounded Surety's hand,
> And then again at mine.[1]

Without Penal Substitution, the logical basis for these doctrines is gone.

In a similar way, the doctrine of unconditional eternal security[2] is also supported by Penal Substitution. If Christ died to pay your debt, then when you accept that payment, the debt is paid off. Paid off debts cannot be reinstated. If you no longer owe any debt to justice, and God always sees Christ's righteousness when he looks at you (rather than your personal unholiness), how could you fall from grace? Again, this is not biblical, but it is logical—if you accept the Penal Substitution view.

---

[1] Augustus Toplady, "From Whence This Fear and Unbelief", 1772. This quote also illustrates the "double jeopardy" that is used to argue limited atonement.
[2] Unconditional eternal security is not a Calvinistic doctrine, but is a modification of Calvin's teaching of the perseverance of the saints. "Perseverance of the saints" implies that the elect person will inevitably persevere, which is usually understood to mean continuing in holiness. "Unconditional eternal security" means if a person has believed on Jesus in the past, he cannot lose his salvation no matter how badly he sins, or how completely he seems to have fallen away,

CHAPTER 3

MORE PROBLEMS WITH PENAL SUBSTITUTION

First, some clarifications

In discussing the Atonement, some careful definitions are needed before we go further. I have already spoken against the ideas that Jesus died to *satisfy* the wrath of God, and that he suffered in our place as a *penal substitute*. However, the terms "satisfaction", "penalty", and "substitute" can all be used in discussing Jesus' death. It is a certain *understanding* of the terms that is to be rejected, not the words themselves.

In Isaiah 53:11, it is said: "Out of the suffering of his soul he will see light and find satisfaction."[1] Jesus was satisfied with the results of his suffering. Of course, the Father, who is one with Jesus,[2] was also satisfied, rejoicing in the redemption that was accomplished. Anselm, departing from the teaching of the church for more than a millennium, taught that Jesus died to make satisfaction for God's lost honor. The Reformers taught that Jesus died to satisfy God's wrath.

Jesus suffered a penalty, or punishment. He challenged the Jewish establishment of his day. They responded by charging

---
[1] ISV
[2] John 10:30

him with blasphemy, and condemned him to death as a criminal. God used this to bring us salvation. "The chastisement [a similar word to punishment] for our peace was upon Him, And by His stripes we are healed."[1] Jesus suffered torture and death on our behalf, and in the process took away our sins. The Father asked him to do this, but it was not God the Father who was punishing him. It was the Jews and Romans.

The word "substitute" has a broad enough range of meanings that it can be used to describe Jesus' death. However, he did not die as a *penal* substitute When theologians put "penal", and "substitution" together into an explanation of the Atonement, they are saying that God's justice needed to be satisfied by punishing sin, so Jesus took God's punishment upon himself. I capitalize Penal Substitution throughout this book to make it clear that I am referring to a specific Atonement theory which makes this claim.

Inasmuch as Jesus did something on our behalf that we could not do for ourselves, (delivering, cleansing, justifying, sanctifying us) he can be seen as our substitute. If I have a broken wrist when it is my turn to bat, and Hank Aaron goes up to bat instead of me, as my substitute, he does something I cannot do for myself.

Penal Substitution lacks historical backing.

Most theological scholars and historians have agreed that no one in the early Church taught Penal Substitution as a primary theory of the atonement. Others, especially recently, disagree.[2]

---

[1] Isaiah 53:5
[2] For example, Jeffrey, Ovey, and Sachs, in *Pierced for Our Transgressions: Rediscovering the Glory of Penal Substitution*, contend that

However, Aulen, in *Christus Victor,* says that when the Latin type (Penal Substitution) Atonement is seen in the early church writings,

> the closest attention needs to be given to the passages in which these phrases and images occur; for it does not by any means follow that the use of legal analogies implies that the writer has in his mind a Latin view of the atonement.[1],[2]

The early Christian view, which can be broadly described as "Christus Victor", taught that Jesus overcame sin, death, and the devil on our behalf.[3] When the early Christians talk about Jesus suffering for our sins, instead of us, it does not follow that they have anything in mind like the modern view of Jesus receiving the Father's wrath and punishment on sin.

Of course, it is possible that no one in the early church understood the Atonement, and it only began to be understood in the time of Anselm with final understanding supplied by the Reformers. But is this likely? Are theologians fifteen centuries removed from the apostles in a better place to understand their writings than those in the second and third centuries? We should hold suspect newer theological ideas that have little or no historical backing.

Penal Substitution was taught in the early Church. In support of this, they quote a number of early Christian writers.

[1] Gustav Aulen, *Christus Victor,* translated by A. G. Hebert, (Eugene, OR, Wipf and Stock Publishers, 2003), 8, 9
[2] Quotes claiming to show the early Christians believed in Penal Substitution are generally misread, or are out of context. As an example, the *Epistle of Mathetes to Diognetus* has a paragraph which defenders of Penal Substitution claim supports their theory ("Oh sweet exchange!"). When this is read in context without importing Penal Substitutionary ideas, this claim disintegrates.
[3] This is the briefest of statements. Much more can be said about this.

Was the debt paid, or forgiven?

Penal Substitution implies that the ultimate reason Jesus came to suffer and die was to satisfy God's wrath, and pay a debt of sin (punishment) that mankind owed God. However, where did Jesus teach this? Where do you find this stated within the New Testament?[1]

Matthew 18 tells the story of a servant who owed a king an enormous debt of ten thousand talents. When he was unable to pay, he pled with his master for mercy and the master forgave him the whole debt. Note that nobody paid the debt on behalf of the servant; it was forgiven! However, this same servant went out and found one of his fellow servants who owed him a small amount, one hundred denarii, and demanded repayment. When the second servant could not pay the debt, the first servant had him cast into prison.

When the master heard of it, he was angry and delivered the first servant to be tortured until he should pay all that he owed. In other words, the master reinstated the debt that he had originally forgiven.[2]

Clearly, the master represents God, and the servants represent his followers. If the debt had been paid off (by Jesus, taking it upon himself), it would have been inappropriate for the king to reinstate it. But because it was forgiven and not paid, that forgiveness only remained as long as the servant acted

---

[1] While there are verses that are taken to be about Jesus satisfying God's wrath, this requires either reading things into them that are not there, or taking a verse in one sense that could easily be taken in another sense.

[2] The king demonstrates his righteousness/justice first by being merciful. Eventually, based on the wicked servant's subsequent actions and lack of appreciation, that same righteousness/justice is demonstrated by casting him into prison.

appropriately in response.[1]

Anselm, in *Cur Deus Homo*, states that God cannot simply forgive sinners because it would be against God's nature to do so. He brings up the fact that Jesus says we are to forgive those who trespass against us.[2] So why would God not do the same? Anselm's answer is that vengeance belongs to God alone; hence he commands us to forgive[3] even while he himself does not forgive without repayment. In other words, God commands us to forgive, but he cannot simply do so without receiving payment for his offended honor.[4]

Anselm's arguments are large on logic and small on Scripture. Otherwise he may have noticed that the reason we are commanded to forgive is so that we can be forgiven likewise,[5] and ultimately so that we can be in character like God.[6] Jesus said, "Therefore, be merciful, *just as* your Father is also merciful."[7]

Under Penal Substitution, the penalty (debt or price) for sin is owed to the Father. However, this penalty can be seen as the natural consequence of sin. When we read "in the day that you eat of it you shall surely die"[8] or "the soul who sins shall die"[9] or "the wages of sin is death,"[10] the Penal Substitution framework interprets this as meaning, "The soul who sins shall be killed by God." A more natural reading would be "the soul

---

[1] David Bercot: *What the Early Christians Believed About the Atonement*, audio CD, Amberson, PA, Scroll Publishing, August 8, 2006.
[2] Matthew 6:12
[3] Jesus' followers cannot take vengeance. Matthew 5:39.
[4] St. Anselm, *The Works of St. Anselm, Cur Deus Homo,* Translated by Sidney Norton Dean, Book 1, Chap. 12, Sacred Texts, accessed April, 2020. http://www.sacred-texts.com/chr/ans/ans117.htm
[5] Matthew 6:14, 15
[6] Matthew 5:45, 48
[7] Matthew 6:36, emphasis added
[8] Genesis 2:17
[9] Ezekiel 18:20
[10] Romans 6:23

who sins shall suffer death as a natural consequence of sin."

If we accept the idea that Jesus paid our penalty, the whole idea of God's mercy is in jeopardy. If he was unable or unwilling to forgive our sins without receiving payment, how is he merciful?[1] The testimony of Scripture is that our debt to God is forgiven, not paid off.

Penal Substitution implies that God was just in bringing wrath on Jesus.

If Jesus had our sins put on him in such a way that God could bring his wrath on Jesus, you would think that in some way this was a just action. Wouldn't it be strange then for God to be angry with those who perpetrated the crucifixion of Jesus? In other words, if Jesus' death was God's just wrath coming down upon him, how could God then have wrath left over for those who killed him?

In fact, many verses indicate that the crucifixion *brought* God's wrath upon those responsible, rather than appeasing God's wrath. Here are some examples:

In a parable, Jesus said:

> But when the king heard about it, he was furious. And he sent out his armies, destroyed those murderers, and burned up their city.[2]

Paul spoke of the Judeans. It was they, he said:

> who killed both the Lord Jesus and their own prophets,

---

[1] Faustus Socinus. *De Jesu Christus Servatore, Part III.* Translated by Alan Gomes, 135.
[2] Matthew 22:7

> and have persecuted us; and they do not please God and are contrary to all men, forbidding us to speak to the Gentiles that they may be saved, so as always to fill up the measure of their sins; but wrath has come upon them to the uttermost.[1]

These passages, among others,[2] illustrate that the crucifixion of Jesus was a wicked act that brought God's wrath.

Penal Substitution makes God's mercy subservient to his retributive justice.

Many people have gotten the idea that ultimately, "God is not merciful. God is just." This opinion does not come from the Bible but is rather based on the tenants of Penal Substitution, which presupposes that God's mercy cannot be fully expressed until his justice is satisfied.

This is the inverse of God's description of himself. God revealed himself to Moses as:

> The Lord, the Lord God, merciful and gracious, longsuffering, and abounding in goodness and truth, keeping mercy for thousands, forgiving iniquity and transgression and sin . . .[3]

Only when all his qualities of mercy, graciousness, and longsuffering have been stated, he then says that he "will by no means clear the guilty"[4] Punishing the guilty is certainly something he does, but if the sequence tells us anything, he is looking hard for ways to show mercy first.

---

[1] 1 Thessalonians 2:15, 16
[2] See also Acts 3:13-15, Acts 4:10, Acts 5:30-32, Acts 7:52-53, Acts 10:39-40
[3] Exodus 34:6-7
[4] Exodus 34:7, KJV

James had no question which is greater, for he says: "mercy triumphs over judgment."[1]

Although theologians are usually careful to describe God as merciful and his wrath coming down upon Jesus as his love toward us, a common understanding that Penal Substitution produces in non-theologians is that the Father is angry and vengeful, and Jesus is the one on our side.[2] Consequently, Penal Substitution twists our perception of God.

Does the cross show the righteousness *of* the law or *apart from* the law?

Penal Substitution says that Jesus had to die because someone had to fulfill the law's requirement, "The soul who sins shall die."[3] Thus, Jesus' death would be demonstrating the righteousness *of the law*.

In contrast, Paul says that Jesus and his work reveal "the righteousness of God apart from the law."[4] In other words, while the law's requirement is righteous, God has another way of revealing righteousness totally apart from working through the legal channels of the Mosaic law! This righteousness apart from the Mosaic law is demonstrated by Jesus Christ.

A defense of Penal Substitution often centers on a misreading of Romans 3:21-26, the passage that tells us that Jesus reveals God's righteousness *apart from the law*. I will quote it in the NRSV, which may be a bit easier to understand than some other translations:

---

[1] James 2:13
[2] N.T. Wright, *The Day the Revolution Began: Reconsidering the Meaning of Jesus' Crucifixion* (San Francisco, HarperOne, 2016), 39, 42.
[3] Ezekiel 18:20
[4] Romans 3:21

> But now, apart from law, the righteousness of God has been disclosed, and is attested by the law and the prophets, the righteousness of God through faith in Jesus Christ for all who believe. For there is no distinction, since all have sinned and fall short of the glory of God; they are now justified by his grace as a gift, through the redemption that is in Christ Jesus, whom God put forward as a sacrifice of atonement[1] by his blood, effective through faith. He did this to show his righteousness, because in his divine forbearance he had passed over the sins previously committed; it was to prove at the present time that he himself is righteous and that he justifies the one who has faith in Jesus.[2],

While a detailed exposition of this passage is beyond our scope here, some observations may be helpful.

In brief, the point this passage is intending to convey is that God's righteousness (apart from the law) to which the law and the prophets bore witness, is now revealed by the faith of Jesus Christ.[3] God's righteousness is revealed to all who believe (both Jew and Gentile).[4]

---

[1] The NRSV translates *hilasterion* in verse 25 as "sacrifice of atonement," but has a footnote that it may be translated "place of atonement." The place of atonement is the covering over the Ark of the Covenant (called *kapporet* in Hebrew) which has come into English as "mercy seat," Many feel "mercy seat" is the intended meaning in this passage. Jesus is our mercy seat—the place or means by which we meet God and our salvation is accomplished. Some translate it as *propitiation,* but that contradicts the point of the passage. See Appendix A under "Propitiation / Mercy Seat for a fuller discussion.
[2] Romans 3:21-25, NRSV
[3] Romans 3:22 The KJV has "faith **of** Jesus Christ." The NKJV has "faith **in** Jesus Christ." The difference here is called the *pistis Christou* debate and concerns the question of whether our faith in Christ (objective genitive) is being referred to or whether it is Christ's faithfulness (subjective genitive) that reveals the righteousness of God. In other words, the subjective genitive reading interprets this verse as saying that since Jesus is himself God, he reveals God's righteousness through his (Jesus') faithfulness, which resulted in our salvation.
[4] Romans 3:22

All need the benefits that have been offered through Christ because "all have sinned and fall short of the glory of God."[1] We have been justified by God's graciousness which was shown through Jesus' redemption.[2]

God set Jesus forth as a meeting place (mercy seat)[3] between God and man. This was accomplished by the shedding of Christ's blood, an act of love and mercy which revealed God's righteousness.[4] In order to bring salvation in the present time, God had to pass over sins (rather than immediately punish) that were committed before the time of Christ.

Was God being unjust/unrighteous by passing over sin? No! Now that Jesus has been revealed as the means of dealing with sin (past, present, and future) and can overcome[5] sin through his merciful self-offering, God is justified in not punishing past sins. For those who were faithful in the Old Testament or for those who have now laid hold on Christ, sins have now been dealt with and taken away by Jesus.[6]

Had there been no means by which those sins could be taken away, God would have been unjust to not punish them. But because he knew those sins would be taken away, he was not unjust to delay punishment until the solution was brought, after which there was no longer a need to bring punishment on those sins he had passed over.

The passage is a dense one, but perhaps it is not as dense as it

---

[1] Romans 3:23
[2] Romans 3:24
[3] Romans 3:25. The word *hilasterion* is used, often translated "propitiation" or "expiation," *Hilasterion* is the word the Greek Septuagint used for the covering that was over the Ark of the Covenant. In English, this has been translated as "mercy seat." See Appendix A under "Propitiation / Mercy Seat" for a fuller discussion.
[4] Romans 3:25
[5] By bringing justification and redemption, Romans 3:24.
[6] Romans 3:26

seems. As N. T. Wright has written,

> "It all becomes so complicated," people grumble, when what they really mean is, "I am so used to reading this passage one way that I find it hard to switch and consider other options."[1]

When we step outside the paradigm of Penal Substitution, we can see that this passage is about God's righteousness as expressed in his mercy. He mercifully passed over sins, and then mercifully set Jesus forth as a means of dealing with past sin and making us righteous. In mercy, he "wiped out the handwriting of requirements that was against us,"[2] thus demonstrating his righteousness apart from, or outside the law.

Could Penal Substitution be conceived as just?

Critics have long complained that there is no justice in causing an innocent person to suffer in the place of the guilty. I've previously cited God's words to Ezekiel:

> The soul who sins shall die. . . . The righteousness of the righteous shall be upon himself, and the wickedness of the wicked shall be upon himself.[3]

The Lord stresses that every man will die for his own sin. This is a close parallel to the law of Moses.[4] Punishment belongs to the perpetrator, and must not be directed to another.

We can point to no real-world scenarios to demonstrate that an innocent person suffering could possibly "satisfy" justice. It is certainly possible to suffer in the place of someone else as an

---
[1] N. T. Wright, *The Day the Revolution Began,* 302
[2] Colossians 2:14
[3] Ezekiel 18:20.
[4] See also Deuteronomy 24:16.

act of mercy. But in such a case, we could hardly say that justice has been satisfied.

Further, there has never been any mechanism proposed whereby actual guilt could be transferred; people who believe this simply take it on faith. Although some Scriptures are interpreted to say that our guilt was placed on Jesus, these can be read in other ways that are more consistent with other Scriptures. If these Scriptures can easily be understood in another way, would it be reasonable to cling to explanations that seem illogical and *unjust*?

People who believe that God's wrath is satisfied as long as someone gets punished do not have a picture of a very benevolent and loving God.[1]

The question of whether Penal Substitution is *just* has been a major stumbling block for many. One former Christian who became an agnostic atheist said,

> As I have pointed out in many posts, the idea that the death of an innocent person could justly be substituted for the sins of guilty people makes no sense. It is contrary to human reason and to any human sense of moral justice. This was the final straw that led to my de-conversion from Evangelical Christianity.[2]

The Skeptics Annotated Bible says:

> And in the ultimate injustice, God punishes everyone for someone else's sin [Adam's], and then saves them

---

[1] I don't know of anyone who claims God simply wants to punish someone, or anyone. But what is the difference between that and the thought that God punished the innocent Jesus to satisfy justice?
[2] Ken Pulliam, "Why I De-converted from Evangelical Christianity," Former Fundy, accessed April, 2020.
http://formerfundy.blogspot.com/2010/07/faustus-socinus-on-penal-substitution_29.html

all by killing an innocent victim.[1]

Jesus' death cannot be equal to man's deserved punishment.

The wages of sin is spiritual death, rather than physical death. If the consequence of sin was physical death, and that death paid for sins committed, then every man would have paid for sin by dying physically, and there would be no justification for hell. If the consequence of sin is eternal death, then Jesus would have needed to experience eternal death to have offered some sort of quid pro quo for man's sin. At the least, he would have had to have suffered in hell.

Indeed, some proponents of Penal Substitution claim that he did. However, this is unsupported by Scripture. Jesus bore our sins in his own body on the tree,[2] not in hell. This means he endured our sins committed against his own body.[3] If the wages of sin is spiritual death, how could Jesus pay for our sins by suffering physical death? Furthermore, the Bible nowhere says that the wages of sin is torture.

Penal Substitution allows for antinomianism.

Faustus Socinus[4] was a Reformation-era critic who raised a

---

[1] "Are We Punished for the Sins of Others?" The Skeptics Annotated Bible, accessed April, 2020. https://skepticsannotatedbible.com/contra/iniquity.html
[2] 1 Peter 2:24
[3] For a fuller discussion of this, see Chapter 11 as well as Appendix B, "1 Peter 2:24".
[4] Socinus raised a number of objections to Penal Substitution, which can be found in *De Jesu Christo Servatore*. This work has never been fully translated. A partial translation can be found at https://www.scribd.com/document/243103401/De-Jesu-Christo-Servatore-Part-III-by-Faustus-Socinus-Trans-Alan-Gomes. Though many of his criticisms are sound, Socinus was a heretic, and some of his criticisms reflect his heretical views.

number of objections to Penal Substitution.[1] Among these, he argued that:

> a perfect substitutionary satisfaction, could such a thing be, would necessarily confer on us unlimited permission to continue in sin.[2]

This is a logical conclusion of the claim that Jesus took our punishment.

The justification of the individual that is proposed by Penal Substitution is called "forensic justification." This basically means that a man is *declared* just/righteous, rather than *made* just/righteous. Here is how Charles Hodge said it:

> ... justification, instead of being an efficient act changing the inward character of the sinner, is a declarative act, announcing and determining his relation to the Law and justice of God.[3]

Hodge's statement, therefore, says that justification is external to the sinner and thus it does not cause a change his inward character. It is then quite an easy jump to say that obedience is therefore optional because inward righteousness is not what God is looking for.

We need to be made righteous, not merely declared righteous. The Greek term meaning "to justify" (*dikaioo*) can equally be

---

[1] According to J. I. Packer, Socinus arraigned Penal Substitution as "irrational, incoherent, immoral and impossible." (J.I. Packer, "What did the Cross Achieve? The Logic of Penal Substitution")
[2] (Ibid.) This is J.I. Packers description of what Socinus said.
[3] Charles Hodge, "Justification Is a Forensic Act," A Puritan's Mind, accessed April 18, 2020. https://www.apuritansmind.com/justification/justification-is-a-forensic-act-by-dr-charles-hodge/

translated "to make righteous."[1]

Penal Substitution lends itself to individualism.

In the Western worldview, law is thought of differently than in Jewish (biblical) thought. In Jewish thought, law is the expression of God's intention for relationships within the community. Forgiveness, repentance, and restitution are all required to maintain relationships among individuals and between individuals and God, so covenant law described how to operate to maintain these relationships. Our Western concepts of law have their origins in Roman law, which was primarily a system of rewards and especially punishments.[2]

The Christian church, defaulting toward Roman conceptions of law, lost the focus of law as a reflection of God's intentions for covenantal relationships and instead saw law as a system for just reward and equivalent retribution (punishment). This can tend to make people lose focus on how they have hurt God and people (and thereby damaged relationships), by instead focusing on the fact that they are headed for punishment because of their sin.

Thus, it is easy for us to lose focus on our need for restoration and wholeness, as well as the need for the redemption of all creation, and instead focus on our problem of guilt.[3] The problem of guilt is real.[4] However, we should be more concerned about the fact that we have slighted and done insult to God and man than about the fact that payday is coming. Penal Substitution is a Western answer to this problem of guilt.

---

[1] See Strong's 1344: https://biblehub.com/greek/1344.htm. Also *TDNT, Vol I*, p.211, says, *dikaioo* ... means "to make righteous, or ... "to establish as right," "to validate".
[2] Driver, John. *Understanding the Atonement For the Mission of the Church*, 32.
[3] Driver, 32-34
[4] The problem of guilt refers to culpability, not feelings of guilt.

It makes salvation available on a very individual basis; the individual works his problem out with God.

The New Testament emphasis is much less on an individualistic salvation. While our need to escape from judgment is acknowledged, the New Testament instead focuses more on the lostness of humanity, our inability to do as we should, and our consequent need to be redeemed.[1]

For Anselm and Aquinas, redemption means freedom from debt or penalty. In the New Testament, however, redemption is described as freedom from slavery.[2]

In the Old Testament, sacrifices are about obedience to God and reconciliation with Him. The Jews did not have the idea that wrath was being poured out upon the sacrificial animal, and it was therefore taking someone's punishment.[3] Rather, God was pleased by the self-sacrifice of the individual in giving up his best animal, and blood was needed for cleansing. The smell of a burnt offering (animal or grain) that was willingly given was a sweet aroma to the Lord. We do not read that the squeals of a tortured animal were sweet music to his ears.[4]

Penal Substitution reduces God's work to an individual level rather than a plan to set right and restore the creation from the fall, which includes us and our salvation along with it. Faith is seen as adherence to a set of doctrinal beliefs, not a faithfulness to God that allows his work in us and brings life into conformity with God's all-encompassing plan. Individualism works against relationships. Redemption restores relationships. Salvation is a rescue from our fallen, sinful state, and results in the restoration of relationships with God, other humans, and

---

[1] Driver. 56
[2] Driver. 58
[3] Driver, 107, 57
[4] The Jewish method of slitting the throat of a sacrificial animal was the most painless way they had to kill it.

even with nature.

Penal Substitution minimizes the incarnation and resurrection.

Penal Substitution places most of the focus on Jesus' death, little on his incarnation, and none on his resurrection. Yet Paul tells us that "we shall be saved by His life."[1] The apostles were continually speaking of his resurrection. We don't want to minimize the importance of his death in accomplishing atonement, but what the apostles were really excited about was the fact that Jesus had risen again and was alive! By this he proved that he was the victor over death and the grave, and showed that he was the real King.

Did God's mind need to be changed, or did ours?

Penal Substitution implies that God needed to be changed. He (his wrath) was unfavorable to us. Jesus, by offering himself, satisfied God's wrath. This is saying that God needed to be reconciled to *us*. But notice how Paul described it: "God was in Christ reconciling the world to Himself."[2]

It was the world that needed reconciled to God (not God to the world), because we were at enmity with him. He made the first move to show his love by proclaiming peace on earth, and goodwill toward men,[3] as demonstrated by sending his son Jesus.

We can see God's plea that we turn from our enmity against

---

[1] Romans 5:10
[2] 2 Corinthians 5:19
[3] Luke 2:14

him in these verses:

> ... we implore you on Christ's behalf, be reconciled to God.[1]

> For it pleased the Father that in Him all the fullness should dwell, and by Him to reconcile all things to Himself. . .[2]

It was not God who was far off and needed to be moved. It was us.

> But now in Christ Jesus you who once were far off have been brought near by the blood of Christ.[3]

It is true that those who are enemies of God can expect his wrath towards them. But as soon as they surrender, they can share in his favor toward those who turn from their rebellion. God has never needed to have his heart changed to be able to receive those who come to him. God is "slow to anger," but as he is continually rejected, his anger builds. Those who ultimately reject him should expect his wrath and righteous judgment against them.

Penal Substitution obscures the character of God.

We become like the gods we worship. Is it a coincidence that the parts of the United States that have the strongest Evangelical Christian presence also tend to have the strongest support for the death penalty?[4] Historically, the majority in

---

[1] 2 Corinthians 5:20
[2] Colossians 1:19-20
[3] Ephesians 2:13
[4] I am not speaking for or against the death penalty. Romans 13:4 teaches that God has given the power of retributive justice to the state for the purpose of putting a restraint on evil and lawlessness. The Christian is called to not

these places have a worldview that is shaped by Penal Substitution, a theory in which retributive justice must be satisfied. The teachings of Jesus as given in the Sermon on the Mount do not fit well into this paradigm. Jesus not only taught us to love our enemies, forgive, and show mercy, but he was the supreme example of it on the cross as we sinned against him. If instead, the cross was God exacting vengeance on sin rather than mercifully enduring it, we lose much of our basis for understanding the message of Jesus.

The view held by the historic Christian church was one where evil was overcome by willingly suffering, and where one turns the other cheek without retaliation.[1] This view does not fit well with Penal Substitution. Suffering love (i.e. peacemaking[2]) and Penal Substitution have never been sustained together very well.

---

exercise retributive justice, but rather to display God's grace and mercy to the world (2 Corinthians 5:18).
[1] Matthew 5:39
[2] Also known as "non-resistance"

CHAPTER 4

IMPUTED RIGHTEOUSNESS

If Jesus died as a penal substitute, a way is needed to apply the benefits of his death to us. The Reformers taught that the merits of Jesus' death are applied to us though the mechanism of imputed righteousness, also called "imputation". Under this teaching, Jesus' righteousness is imputed to us; but this does not imply that the sinner is actually made righteous. Rather, he is *declared* righteous even though he is not. While "imputed" actually means "credited" or "counted", the prevailing Protestant understanding of imputation understands it as a transfer. Accordingly, it is understood that our sins were counted (transferred) to Christ, and then when we believe on him, his righteousness is counted (transferred) to our account.

Thus, in this view, the sinner is not changed. Instead, it is simply his status before God that is changed.

R.C. Sproul says it this way:

> When we say that the Reformation view of justification is synthetic, we mean that when God declares a person to be just in His sight, it is not because of what He finds in that person under His analysis. Rather, it is on the basis of something that is added to the person. That something that is added, of course, is the righteousness

of Christ. This is why Luther said that the righteousness by which we are justified is *extra nos*, meaning 'apart from us' or 'outside of us.'[1]

The righteousness of Christ that is imputed (counted) to us is said to be alien, that is, completely external. R. C. Sproul continues:

> [Luther] also called it an 'alien righteousness,' not a righteousness that properly belongs to us, but a righteousness that is foreign to us, alien to us. It comes from outside the sphere of our own behavior.[2]

Sproul says God does not declare a person to be righteous on the basis of anything he finds in that person. Instead (according to Sproul) God declares a person to be righteous on the basis of Christ's righteousness transferred to the person's account. This seems rather odd when compared to the way Paul uses the word "imputed."[3] Paul states that God imputed (counted) Abraham as righteous because of *Abraham's* faith.[4] Was Abraham's faith not something that was *in* him?

Because under Penal Substitution, man's problem with God is primarily seen as a legal one, a legal way is needed to apply Jesus' death to our account. Sproul explains this as follows:

> Of course, Protestantism really teaches a double imputation. Our sin is imputed to Jesus and His righteousness is imputed to us. In this twofold transaction, we see that God does not compromise His

---

[1] R.C. Sproul, "The Very Heart of the Reformation." Ligonier, accessed April, 2020, https://www.ligonier.org/blog/very-heart-reformation/
[2] Sproul.
[3] Romans 4:9-25
[4] While "imputed" means "reckoned", Protestant thought communicates it in the sense of being transferred, hence if Christ's righteousness was reckoned to us, that could imply a transfer. However, if Abraham's own faith is reckoned as righteousness, there is no transfer happening.

> integrity in providing salvation for His people. Rather, He punishes sin fully after it has been imputed to Jesus. This is why He is able to be both 'just and the justifier of the one who has faith in Jesus,' as Paul writes in Romans 3:26. So, my sin goes to Jesus and His righteousness comes to me.[1]

Sproul considers this to be a defining feature of the Protestant Reformation:

> This is a truth worth dividing the church. This is the article on which the church stands or falls, because it is the article on which we all stand or fall.[2]

So to Sproul, this interpretation of imputation is the very heart of the Reformation. He is even willing to say that the Protestant doctrine of imputation is worth dividing the church over!

John Piper agrees with this interpretation of how Christ's righteousness benefits us:

> We "become" God's righteousness the way Christ "was made" our sin. *He* did not become morally sinful in the imputation; *we* do not become morally righteous in the imputation. *He* was counted as having our sin; *we* are counted as having God's righteousness. This is the reality of imputation. And the righteousness imputed is not our faith but an external divine righteousness.[3]

Notice carefully—Piper is saying that our sins were counted to Christ, but he did not become morally sinful. Since (in his view) this is a quid pro quo, when Christ's righteousness is

---

[1] R.C. Sproul, "The Very Heart of the Reformation."
[2] Sproul.
[3] John Piper, *Counted Righteous in Christ*, 69. Accessed 12/13/19, https://document.desiringgod.org/counted-righteous-in-christ-en.pdf?ts=1439242054

counted to us, *we do not become morally righteous as a result.* The righteousness is external.

Piper and other advocates of Penal Substitution may have other categories under which they talk about the righteousness of a Christian (namely sanctification), but they teach that this is unrelated to our standing with Christ or God's declaration that a person is righteous.[1]

J. I. Packer agrees with Piper and Sproul in his understanding of how Jesus' death saves us. He says:

> Our sins were reckoned (imputed) to Christ, so that he bore God's judgment on them, and in virtue of this his righteousness is reckoned ours, so that we are pardoned, accepted, and given a righteous man's status for his sake. Christians in themselves are sinners who never fully meet the law's demands; nonetheless, says Luther, "they are righteous because they believe in Christ, whose righteousness covers them and is imputed to them."[2]

A legal relationship or a personal relationship?

As you read the Protestant view of imputed righteousness, did you notice how very legal it all sounded? It certainly does not sound very personal. In this construct, God's mercy is

---

[1] Most proponents of this stress that works are a *result* of faith, and that if faith is not demonstrated by works, that proves there was no faith at all. However, the way this is emphasized often results in good works being seen negatively, as something dangerous because we are so prone to get the wrong ideas about them. The apostle James has the opposite concern; he wants to ensure that we understand that we are not justified by faith alone, but by works also (James 2:24). This will be explored further in chapter five.

[2] J.I. Packer, "Sola Fide: The Reformed Doctrine of Justification. Ligonier.org. Accessed 12/13/19, https://www.ligonier.org/learn/articles/sola-fide-the-reformed-doctrine-of-justification/

expressed once, in the past, by "signing" a legal document of sorts that declares we are acquitted because Jesus was punished instead. So whenever I might feel a doubt about my salvation or some sort of insecurity about my relationship with God, I appeal to this legal status. But legal agreements between two parties are not *in and of themselves* based on genuine relationships.

This is a view of a God who cannot forgive but must punish the smallest sin. Thus, as long as the smallest sin could be attributed to me, I must despair of any hope of salvation. This view *claims* to be taking sin very seriously.[1] What happens instead is that sin is trivialized:[2]

> If the smallest sin on my part is deserving of God's eternal unquenchable wrath, then God is so impossible to placate that I need not work out my salvation with fear and trembling. Salvation can at that point only rest on whether I think the right things about the atonement and not on whether I am surrendering my life to Jesus Christ. If the smallest wrong thought is worthy of eternal damnation, then sin hardly comes in greater and lesser degrees.[3]

However, Jesus clearly said that some sins are greater than others.[4]

This legal view of our relationship with God is demonstrated

---

[1] When Boso asked Anselm why God cannot show mercy (without receiving payment) when someone repents, Anselm replied, "You have not yet weighed the gravity of sin." *Cur Deus Homo* Book 1, Chap 21.
[2] I remember a conversation in which a man was telling a friend and me about how he cheats at the toll booth. He would put his hat (which was the same color as his weight class sticker) under the sticker. The toll booth agent couldn't see the sticker well and would often assess him as a lower weight class. My friend called him out on this and the man replied, "I tell you what, the Lord Jesus is up there forgiving *my* sin!"
[3] Anthony Hess, personal email to author, 12/10/2019
[4] John 19:11

by a question Protestants have often asked. "When you stand before God, and he asks, 'Why should I let you into heaven?' what will you say?" The correct answer is supposed to be, "Because of the merits of Jesus Christ alone!"

This is a terrible question, and a flawed answer. Would you ask such a question of one of your friends before letting him into your house? Certainly not if he is your friend! I expect to spend eternity with God because I know he is faithful, because he loves me, and I love him. Based on his love and what I know of his character, he would never put one of his friends in hell.

I rest in his promise that if I confess my sins, he is faithful and just to forgive me and cleanse me from all unrighteousness.[1]

Our relationship to God

How should we think biblically about sin? Sin is deadly.[2] No sin can be excused.[3] All sin should be repented of and grieved over.[4] But we need to understand that the basis of our acceptance with God is in our *relationship* to him.

The picture God has given us to understand our relationship to him is that of a husband and wife.[5] Of course, there is a certain legal component in my marriage relationship because one day years ago, I made a solemn promise to my wife to love, cherish, forgive, and provide for her until death. Nothing can make me break this promise. No matter what happens, I will keep it. The only thing that can break our relationship is if my

---

[1] John 1:9
[2] Romans 8:13, James 1:15
[3] James 1:13-14
[4] 2 Corinthians 7:9-10
[5] Ephesians 5:22-33

wife leaves. Even then, I would remain faithful to her by not breaking *my* vows in finding another wife. Only she could break our relationship.[1]

However, I don't spend that much time thinking about our wedding and the promises I made. The memory remains, but the basis of my relationship with my wife is our daily commitment to love one another and work together. Because of this, we keep working on our relationship through thick and thin. We forgive. We love. My wife has faults.[2] Some I address. Others I overlook. I may tell her fondly that she is the perfect wife. But how odd it would be to say, "The only way we can have a relationship is if I declare you to be flawless on the basis of my perfection, which I substitute for your faults"!

Our relationship with God starts with a covenant to him. We make this covenant with him because we want to be in relationship with him. He begins to share his qualities with us, making us into the "perfect wife." Our relationship with God is based on his love and mercy. This is not just a past mercy when he imputed Jesus' righteousness to our account, but an ongoing mercy, where he loves us because he is loving and faithful. He continues to transform us. As long as our hearts are turned towards him, we continue in that mercy. Because he is faithful, we need not fear as long as we continue in love. Only we could terminate that relationship (by leaving him).[3] However, if we are unmerciful to others, it isn't possible for us

---

[1] In our human relationship, it is possible that I could be the one who leaves and is unfaithful to my promise. However, I am using this analogy to describe how our relationship with God works. In our relationship with God, we have the assurance that God will never be the unfaithful party. 2 Timothy 2:13 says, "If we are faithless, He remains faithful; He cannot deny Himself."

[2] I am using this solely as a picture of Christ and the church. In that relationship, I am the wife who has many faults (and in my earthly marriage, I also have many faults).

[3] 2 Timothy 2:13

to receive his mercy.[1]

Effects of the Protestant Doctrine of Imputation

John Wesley saw the effects of the Protestant doctrine of imputation. He said,

> I have known very many who so rested in the doctrine of the righteousness of Christ imputed to them, that they were quite satisfied without any holiness at all. . . .[2]

Further, he said, this doctrine is

> "A blow at the root," the root of all holiness, all true religion. Hereby Christ is "stabbed in the house of his friends," of those who make the largest professions of loving and honouring him; the whole design of his death, namely, "to destroy the works of the devil," being overthrown at a stroke. For wherever this doctrine is cordially received, it leaves no place for holiness.[3]

Wesley was unable to find the phrase "the imputing [of] the righteousness of Christ" in the Bible.

> I cannot find it in the Bible. If anyone can, he has better eyes than I: and I wish he would show me where it is.[4]

Wesley believed "the righteousness of God" refers to his mercy

---

[1] James 2:13
[2] John Wesley, *"The Works of the Reverend John Wesley, A. M.* published by J. Emory and B. Waugh, J Collard Printer, 1831, 181, accessed February 5, 2020. https://archive.org/details/03553688.1116.emory.edu/page/n1/mode/2up
[3] John Wesley, *"The Works of the Reverend John Wesley, A. M.* 138.
[4] Wesley, 102.

and his means of justifying sinners.[1] But he said the phrase "imputed righteousness of Christ" is not there and should be dropped. Now, Christ is righteous, but in Protestant theological speak, the term "righteousness of Christ" is used to refer to an idea that Christ has merits that are legally transferred to our account.

> ... And I have frequently used the phrase [imputed righteousness], hoping thereby to please others, for their good to edification. But it has had a contrary effect, since so many improve it into an objection. Therefore I will use it no more (I mean, the phrase Imputed Righteousness: that phrase, the Imputed Righteousness of Christ, I never did use.) I will endeavour to use only such phrases as are strictly Scriptural. And I will advise all my brethren, all who are in connection with me throughout the three kingdoms, to lay aside that ambiguous, unscriptural phrase (the Imputed Righteousness of Christ), which is so liable to be misinterpreted, and speak in all instances, this in particular, as the oracles of God.[2]

Biblical Imputation

I agree with John Wesley that the idea that Christ's righteousness is credited to our account is not taught in the Bible. Christ's righteousness was not imputed to Abraham. Instead, the Bible[3] tells us that Abraham's *own* faith was imputed (counted) as righteousness, and the same can be true

---

[1] *"The righteousness of Christ is an expression which I do not find in the Bible. "The righteousness of God" is an expression which I do find there. I believe this means, first, The Mercy of God ... I believe this expression means, Secondly, God's method of justifying sinners."* Wesley, 100-101.
[2] Wesley, p. 182
[3] Genesis 15:6 and Romans 4:3

for us. There is no transfer of righteousness from someone else here.

Paul uses the word "impute" in his letter to the Romans.

> Even as David also describeth the blessedness of the man, unto whom God imputeth righteousness without works.[1]

Because we have been taught how to understand this from a Penal Substitution point of view, we imagine some legal transaction where Christ's righteousness is transferred to us and our sin is transferred to him. However, the Bible teaches that one person's guilt cannot be counted against someone else, and neither can one person's righteousness be counted for someone else.[2]

Rather than saying that Christ's righteousness is imputed to our account, this passage says if we have faith, God counts (imputes) us as righteous! We are counted as righteous if we believe on Jesus, because believing enables him to change our hearts in the new birth.[3] We are counted as unrighteous if we do not believe on Jesus (even if we are perfectly keeping the ceremonial law as Saul was before his conversion) because if we have not believed, our hearts have not yet been changed. So, shall we throw out the concept of being declared righteous altogether? No indeed! God's declaration that a man is righteous is a precious truth.

---

[1] Romans 4:6 KJV
[2] Deuteronomy 24:16, Jeremiah 31:30, Ezekiel 18:20
[3] True believing means that one is putting one's trust in God. This requires an acceptance of the truth about myself (repentance) and a resolve to follow God. Take away repentance or obedience, and one is not believing (putting faith in) in the biblical sense.

Declared Righteousness

Righteousness, or the lack thereof, is shown by our actions. We cannot really know if someone is righteous until we have observed them react to positive and negative situations enough to see what is coming out in their responses. However, God knows the heart. He knows if a person has the kind of heart disposition that will lead to righteousness. This heart disposition that will lead to righteousness is called "faith." If God sees faith in the heart, he does not need to wait until the person demonstrates it in righteous acts to declare that the person is righteous. God knows what will be the result.

When Abraham believed God, God looked into his heart and saw trust in God there. God counts that kind of heart attitude as righteous even if no righteous works have yet happened. So "Abraham believed God, and it was accounted to him for righteousness."[1]

God *knew* that Abraham's faith was the kind that *would lead to* righteousness, so he declared Abraham to be righteous before Abraham demonstrated it in action. Praise the Lord for his kindness!

James tells us that Abraham's faith was made perfect (complete) by his works.[2] In other words, God had declared Abraham to be righteous,[3] and Abraham demonstrated that this was true by being willing to offer up Isaac. So first, Abraham was justified (declared/made to be just) by his faith. Then later, he was justified (declared/shown) to be just by his works. That is why James can say, "You see then that a man is justified by works [also], and not by faith only."[4]

---

[1] Romans 4:3
[2] James 2:22
[3] About 50 years earlier! Genesis 15:6
[4] James 2:24

When a sinful man turns from his sin and gives himself to God, his heart is changed. In spite of the fact that his past is marred by sin, God counts him as righteous. This is a great blessing! It is why David says:

> Blessed are those whose lawless deeds have been forgiven, And whose sins have been covered. Blessed is the man whose sin the Lord will not take into account.[1]

The repentant man does not have to be able to go back and fix everything he ruined before he is counted as righteous. He does not have to balance his past evil with a certain amount of good works before he is counted as righteous. He is counted as righteous the moment he lays down his self and makes Jesus his Lord. The thief on the cross had no opportunity to make amends for the past. But he trusted in Christ, and on the basis of his faith, God counted him as righteous. Because God is righteous, he is merciful. And in mercy, he forgives the repentant sinner without requiring any payment be made!

Ultimately, true righteousness comes from the heart.

> For I delight in the law of God according to the inward man.[2]

> Put on the new man which was created according to God, in true righteousness and holiness.[3]

Because the heart represents the core of your personality, what is in your heart is who you truly are. If you are brain damaged so that you cannot move, cannot speak, cannot perform any righteous acts – cannot do anything – but you have a heart full of faith and love for Jesus, you are righteous. Righteousness may be seen in external actions, but righteousness itself is more

---

[1] Romans 4:7, 8 NASB
[2] Romans 7:22
[3] Ephesians 4:24

than actions.

On the other hand, if you perfectly discipline your speech and actions to conform to the Mosaic law, but you have hatred and wickedness in your heart, you are unrighteous. This is because who *you* are, your heart, is wicked. This is what Paul means when he says that righteousness is not by the works of the law. No matter how many apparently righteous deeds you do, if your heart is wicked, you are wicked. It is why Paul says,

> And though I bestow all my goods to feed the poor, and though I give my body to be burned, but have not love, it profits me nothing.[1]

Unfortunately, many people get suspicious any time someone says that good works are important. They feel that somehow, the teaching of salvation by grace through faith is being threatened. The remedy to this is not to downplay good works, but to recognize in humility that all good within us comes from God. Jesus said, "without me, you can do nothing."[2]

If we grasp a hold of this, we will give God the credit for any good we do. Paul says,

> For we are His workmanship, created in Christ Jesus for good works, which God prepared beforehand that we should walk in them.[3]

Paul refers to Christ's workmanship in us as "the righteousness which is through faith in Christ. "[4]

This is not Christ's merit imputed to our account without changing us. Instead, it is the righteousness that Christ works in

---

[1] 1 Corinthians 13:3
[2] John 15:5
[3] Ephesians 2:10
[4] Philippians 3:9

us as we yield our lives to him. Paul says furthermore that we cannot produce this righteousness ourselves; nor will keeping the Mosaic law produce it. Paul's desire is

> That I may . . . be found in Him, not having my own righteousness, which is from the law, but that which is through faith in Christ[1].

It is God's work in us; all the glory belongs to him.

The doctrine of imputed righteousness as put forth by the Reformers has given many people a false sense of security. They gave a mental assent to certain beliefs about Jesus and were told they were saved, even though they continued in their sin. At the judgment, sadly, such people will be told, "I never knew you: depart from me, ye that work iniquity."[2]

---

[1] Philippians 3:8-9
[2] Matthew 7:23 KJV

CHAPTER 5

FAITH

The New Testament stresses the importance of faith in our relationship to God. Jesus said, "whoever believes [*exercises faith*] in Him should not perish but have everlasting life."[1]

Paul told the church of Ephesus, "For by grace you have been saved through faith."[2] And he told the Corinthian believers, "For we walk by faith, not by sight".[3]

In the Old Testament, faith is described by the Hebrew word *emunah*. This word has a primary meaning of "faithfulness," and is a term that can describe God. For example, "Your faithfulness [*emunah*] endures to all generations."[4]

Interestingly, *emunah* is only once translated as "faith" (rather than "faithfulness")[5]. In Habakkuk 2:4 we read, "the just shall live by his faith."

Considering that *emunah* is translated as "faithful*ness*" elsewhere, why is not this verse translated as "The just shall live

---

[1] John 3:15
[2] Ephesians 2:8
[3] 2 Corinthians 5:7
[4] Psalm 119:90
[5] In the KJV

by his faithful*ness*" also?[1]

When Paul quotes this verse,[2] he uses the Greek word *pistis* which can mean either "faith" or "faithfulness." For theological and contextual reasons, *pistis* is often translated as "faith" including in each instance where Paul quotes Habakkuk. This is such an important theme for Paul that the translation "faith" is read back into the Old Testament source.

Now it's quite interesting *how* Paul quotes this verse. Each of the three times he quotes it, he drops the word "his." Hence, "The just shall live by faith." What is Paul's warrant for dropping the word "his"?

Paul was quite familiar with both the Hebrew Scriptures and the Septuagint (Greek) translation of them. In the Septuagint, the text reads, "The just shall live by *My* faithfulness."[3] Thus, in the Septuagint, it is *God's* faithfulness that the righteous person lives by.

So Paul has a textual problem. Is Habakkuk referring to our faith (Masoretic) or to God's faithfulness (Septuagint)? Paul brilliantly solves this dilemma by making it to be both! He drops both the *his* and the *My*, and says, "The just shall live by faith(fulness)." Now, both God's part in this and our part are included in one statement.

Before you dismiss this proposal, let's look at the context of Paul's quote of this in Romans 1:17:

> For in it [the gospel] the righteousness of God is revealed *from faith to faith*; as it is written, the just shall

---

[1] The context of Habakkuk 2:4 is that judgment is coming, but the righteous one will be spared because of his faithfulness.
[2] Romans 1:17, Galatians 3:11, Hebrews 10:38 (Paul's authorship of Hebrews is disputed.)
[3] It could be "My faith," but since it is God's *emunah* (translated *pistis*), "faithfulness" is a better translation.

live by faith.[1]

Now as I have said, "faith" is translated from the Greek word *pistis*. The English word "faith" usually refers to trust, which *could* be understood as primarily a mental belief. However, the Greek word for faith (*pistis*) can also refer to faithfulness (fidelity).[2]

So what does "from faith to faith" mean? Paul is communicating both aspects of the Hebrew and Greek in Habakkuk 2:4. In the gospel, God's righteousness is revealed from *his faithfulness* to *our faith*.[3] Paul is trying to portray that the just one lives by his faith, and by God's faithfulness.

Now, because *pistis* can mean both "faith" and "faithfulness", Paul can use it to mean either/or, or both at the same time. When applied to God, the most understandable translation is "faithfulness." For example, in Romans 3:3, the "*pistis* of God" is best understood as the *faithfulness* of God, hence, "Will their unbelief make the faithfulness of God without effect?"[4]

Pistis can also refer to human faithfulness. Considering the context, Romans 1:5 is most logically translated "obedience of faithfulness."

> Through Him we have received grace and apostleship for obedience *of faithfulness* among all nations for His name.[5]

Here's another example where *pistis* here is most naturally

---

[1] Romans 1:17 emphasis added
[2] In English, the word "faith" can also be used to refer to faithfulness. Someone may be said to have "acted in good faith" (faithfully). Or you might say, "Keep faith!" but in modern English we would generally say, "Be faithful!"
[3] Or "our faithfulness."
[4] Romans 3:3
[5] Romans 1:5, altered from the New King James version

translated as "faithfulness:"[1]

> I thank my God . . . hearing of your love and *faithfulness* which you have toward the Lord Jesus and toward all the saints.[2]

Often, context illustrates that the better translation of human *pistis* is "faith".[3] However, because Paul uses this word both ways, "faith's" connection to "faithfulness" is natural, and always present in his mind.

However, because "faith" can be taken to refer to a mental attitude, some people take Paul's teaching about faith and strip it of its proper connection to faithfulness. When this happens, they believe that what primarily matters is mental assent to intellectual beliefs about God.

As early as New Testament times, James felt a need to bring clarity to this topic. He wrote to convince his hearers that faith without works was insufficient. He asked, "What does it profit, my brethren, if someone says he has faith but does not have works? Can faith save him?"[4]

James is trying to demonstrate that faith that does not result in righteousness is no faith at all.

There is a reason that Martin Luther referred to the Epistle of James as a "right strawy epistle".[5] Luther taught an understanding of faith *that divorced it from faithfulness.* Luther wrestled much with guilt, anger at what he thought was the

---

[1] *Pistis* is here translated as "faith." However, context shows that "faithfulness" is the better translation, because Philemon has *pistis* toward all the saints. In other words, he is faithful toward Jesus and others.
[2] Philemon 1:4-5, altered
[3] For example, see Luke 7:9, Colossians 1:4, and James 1:6
[4] James 2:14
[5] David Mathis, "The Gospel of James: Open Letter to Martin Luther," Desiring God, accessed December 14, 2019. https://www.desiringgod.org/articles/the-gospel-of-james

harshness of God, and doubts about his salvation. When one realizes what mental anguish he went through in trying to find peace with God, it is easy to see why Luther embraced this idea. But he should have found the true solution to his guilt *in God's vast forgiveness, faithfulness, mercy, and love.* Instead, he found it in a redefined understanding of faith.

Luther explains his faith journey this way:

> For I had hated that phrase, 'the righteousness of God' which, according to the use and custom of all the doctors, I had been taught to understand philosophically, in the sense of the formal or *active righteousness* (as they termed it), by which God is righteous, and punishes unrighteous sinners . . .
>
> I did not love—in fact I hated—that righteous God who punished sinners, if not with silent blasphemy, then certainly with great murmuring. I was angry with God, saying 'As if it were not enough that miserable sinners should be eternally damned through original sin, with all kinds of misfortunes laid upon them by Old Testament law, and yet God adds sorrow upon sorrow through the gospel, and even brings his wrath and righteousness to bear through it!'[1]

Luther's problem here is that he is thinking of the righteousness of God primarily in the sense of God punishing sinners. With such a narrow view of God's righteousness, and feeling himself to be a sinner deserving judgment, he hated God.[2]

His mental agony was solved by coming to a new

---

[1] Alister E. McGrath: *Luther's Theology of the Cross: Martin Luther's Theological Breakthrough.* (Oxford, UK; Malden, MA: Blackwell Publishers, 2000) 96. Emphasis added.
[2] For an explanation of God's righteousness/justice, see Chapter 10 under the heading, "God's justice."

understanding of faith:

> At last, God being merciful . . . I began to understand that 'righteousness of God'. . . to refer to a *passive righteousness*, by which the merciful God justifies us by faith. . . This immediately made me feel as though I had been born again, and as though I had entered through open gates into paradise itself.[1]

Luther thus distinguished between *active* and *passive* righteousness. Active righteousness is righteousness of character, behavior, and attitudes. Passive righteousness (in Luther's view) is righteousness that is alien to us (not in us) and is imputed to us by Jesus. In other words, passive righteousness is external—not internal—righteousness.

You see where this thought is leading? Since Luther believed God would condemn man if he were to judge a man's active righteousness, then God must judge on the basis of something else. And that something else is passive righteousness, imputed (counted) to us if we believe in Jesus.

In his Galatians lectures of 1516-1517, Luther comments on Galatians 2:16:

> A wonderful new definition of righteousness! This is usually described thus: "Righteousness is a virtue which renders to each man according to his due. . . ." But here it says: "Righteousness is faith in Jesus Christ!"[2]

In other words, Luther is saying that righteousness no longer refers to *being* righteous, but instead refers to *having faith in Jesus*.

---

[1] McGrath, 96-97. Emphasis added.
[2] McGrath, 112

Now, if a person has true saving faith, they will be counted righteous by God. However, with his distinction between active and passive righteousness, Luther separated obedience to God from faith in God. Faith became a mental assent to certain beliefs. This allows a person to be considered to have faith even if their life does not show fruits of it.[1] Luther was trying hard to separate faith from any deeds of righteousness.

The Scriptures clearly teach that we are saved by grace through faith, and this is a precious truth. But it is the kind of faith that James talks about that God is looking for. It is the James kind of faith that results in *faithfulness*[2] that will lead to God's declaration that we are righteous, even as he declared Abraham to be righteous.

In their desperation to drive a wedge between faith and works, the Reformers introduced theological error that continues to bear bad fruit today in many who believe that obedience to Jesus is optional.[3]

So where are we now?

---

[1] Martin Luther may not agree that his articulation of faith allowed for licentiousness. However, this seemed lost on his hearers, as it is demonstrable the Protestant Reformation caused an increase in immorality. For example, he wrote to a friend, "Be a sinner and sin boldly, but believe and rejoice in Christ even more boldly." Debates rage about this statement. Luther has his defenders who explain that he is misunderstood and quoted out of context. But Luther clearly believed something that caused him to make a statement that Jesus or the Apostles would never have said.

[2] James 2:14, 17

[3] A correspondent with *Anabaptist Voice* writes, "The teaching I heard always appeared to me as though it had to be law OR grace, belief OR works; one or the other.... Among my friends, keeping the commandments was always called "works salvation". This fear of being labeled "works Christians" showed in the lives of most Christians I knew, despite the commandments of Jesus and the admonitions of the Apostles to do and not do certain things." ("Finding My Way", *Anabaptist Voice*, no. 13, [Spring 2019]: 41.)

The primary goal of this book has been to expose Penal Substitution as unbiblical. In the process, however, we have talked about the related doctrines of imputed righteousness, and the way the Reformers understood the meaning and role of faith.

In the next chapter we will explore the development of Atonement theology through history, before going on to build a biblical view of the Atonement.

Chapter 6

Atonement Theology in History

The New Testament makes many statements about the work of Christ, and gives us a number of pictures and metaphors to help us understand it. But it does not present a systematic theology of how the Atonement works. Nor did the Early Church develop one. However, while the early Christians did not develop a systematic theology of the Atonement, they left us many writings from which we can glean an understanding of how they viewed the work of Christ.

The Classic Model

It is clear that the early Church Fathers tended to see the Atonement in terms of a cosmic struggle of the kingdom of God against the kingdom of the world (Satan's). In more recent times, this model of the Atonement has been given various labels such as Conflict/Victory, Christus Victor, Classic Dramatic, or simply the Classic Model of the Atonement. We will refer to it as the Classic Model.[1] Christ was thought of as

---

[1] It is debated whether any early Church Fathers taught any form of Penal Substitution. Within the first five centuries, a few quotes suggest similar ideas; however, none seem to have held this as their prevailing explanation. Scholars such as S. J. Romanides believe that these passages should be understood in the

waging warfare on behalf of humanity, and emerging as the victor, triumphing over death, hell and the grave. In early Christian thought, salvation was won on a *battlefield*.

The early Christians believed in concepts such as Ransom, Recapitulation, and Resurrection being involved in the Atonement. Irenaeus gives one of the first and clearest presentations of some of these concepts.[1]

Some of the Fathers focused on the Atonement as a ransom. Within this understanding, at the crucifixion, God offered Christ's life as a ransom payment to attain an objective he desired. Within this view, there was a diversity of opinion on who this ransom was paid to:

- Some understood the ransom as a payment to death itself.

- Others believed that Christ's life was given as a ransom payment to the devil.[2] It was likened to a fish swallowing a worm on a hook; the devil thought he could take Christ a captive in death and hold him there, but did not see the hook lurking in the bait to ensnare him.[3]

- A few spoke of the ransom as a payment to God (although some specifically denied this possibility). Interestingly, even proponents of this view were thinking very differently than the modern idea that God's justice needed to be satisfied. Rather, they were

---

context of rescuing us from the power of sin and death. (Fr. J. S. Romanides [translated by G. S. Gabriel], The Ancestral Sin, Zephyr Publishing, Ridgewood, NJ, 1998)

[1] Gustav Aulen, *Christus Victor*, translated by A. G. Hebert,(Eugene, OR, Wipf and Stock Publishers, 2003), 18-19, 28-29

[2] Aulen, *Christus Victor*, 47-50. also see Athanasius, *On the Incarnation of the Word*, 4.20.

[3] Aulen, 52

> thinking that "deliverance from the powers of evil, death, and the devil is at the same time deliverance from God's judgment on sin."[1]

The idea of Recapitulation was also present in very early times. Irenaeus gave the first clear presentation of this idea (and its necessary counterpart of Christ's incarnation).[2] It was expounded in the fourth century in a work by Athanasius called, *On the Incarnation of the Word*. A modern writer explains:

> Recapitulation teaches that Christ became human to heal mankind by perfectly uniting the human nature to the Divine Nature in His person. Through the Incarnation, Christ took on human nature, becoming the Second Adam, and entered into every stage of humanity, from infancy to adulthood, uniting it to God. He then suffered death to enter Hades and destroy it. After three days, He resurrected and completed His task by destroying death.
>
> By entering each of these stages and remaining perfectly obedient to the Father, Christ recapitulated every aspect of human nature. He said "Yes" where Adam said "No" and healed what Adam's actions had damaged. This enables all of those who are willing to say yes to God to be perfectly united with the Holy Trinity through Christ's person. In addition, by destroying death, Christ reversed the consequence of the fall. Now, all can be resurrected. Those who choose to live their life in Christ can be perfectly united to the Holy Trinity, receiving the full love of God as Heavenly

---

[1] Aulen, 56
[2] Aulen, 16ff., esp. 20-22,29

bliss.[1]

Recapitulation remains the dominant teaching of the Atonement in the Eastern Orthodox church (Protestants inherited Penal Substitution through the stream of Roman Catholicism). Because in Recapitulation, Jesus is said to have healed what Adam damaged, this has been described as God bringing salvation through a *hospital* setting.[2]

The early Christians also emphasized the Resurrection as a vital part of the Atonement.[3] Christ defeated death in the resurrection, and rose as the triumphant victor. The resurrection life and power that he possesses is the source of our life.

The early Christians held these ideas of Ransom, Recapitulation, and Resurrection together, not in exclusion of each other. These themes, with their focus on the fact that Christ's death and resurrection affected a cosmic victory over sin and Satan, form what is known as the Classic Model of the Atonement.

For one thousand years, this Classic Model dominated the church's understanding of the Atonement. During the first several centuries of Christian history, the church stood in radical opposition to the world system. Christians were persecuted and tortured. It was very easy for them to understand themselves as being part of a kingdom that was in radical conflict with earthly kingdoms. In that context, understanding the Atonement in terms of God's conflict with

---

[1] Darrell, "What Is the Eastern Orthodox View of the Atonement," Tough Questions Answered, November 9, 2011, https://www.toughquestionsanswered.org/2011/11/09/the-recapitulation-theory/

[2] Darrell.

[3] E.g. Athanasius, *On the Incarnation of the Word*, chap 5, section 30, chap 4, section 21.

and victory over the powers of evil came naturally.¹

However, as the relationship of the church to culture shifted, change was inevitable. The church gradually merged with the world; the state became "Christian" and the former separation of the church and the world became confused. With Christianity as the dominant religion in the Roman Empire, "Christians" no longer stood in opposition to society. Who was the world? The spiritual focus shifted from the clash of two rival kingdoms to a more individualistic approach: the sinner in relation to God.²

Despite having its foundations undermined, the Classic Model remained the dominant understanding for the first millennium of Christian history. Eventually, however, Christians would no longer be primarily defined as those who are Christlike, but as those who hold to certain doctrinal beliefs. To support that shift in thinking, it would eventually make more sense to understand Christ's work as an:

> abstract 'saving' transaction which allows sinful and violent people . . . and corrupted structures to remain substantially unchanged.³

The Satisfaction theory

In the eleventh century, a very significant development happened when Anselm, the archbishop of Canterbury, explained his views in his book *Cur Deus Homo* (Latin for

---

[1] Western minds have a hard time imagining life in a world filled with temples to false gods. The early Christians identified these as demons, and were persecuted for refusing to worship them. It was only natural for them to emphasize Christ's victory over the devil and his minions, perhaps even to the point of downplaying other aspects of the Atonement.
[2] Driver, 29-30.
[3] Driver, 31.

Why the God-Man?). His views became the basis for what is known as the Satisfaction theory of the Atonement. Anselm drew heavily on concepts that underpinned the feudal system, and may therefore be foreign to our way of thinking and difficult for us to understand. Anselm views man's relation to God in terms of a feudal society in which serfs live on an estate and owe their overlords a debt of honor. When a man sins, he robs honor from God. Having stolen from God, he now is obligated to repay. But like a medieval serf owned nothing, man does not have what he needs to repay God.

> Anselm . . . regarded human sin as defrauding God of the honour he is due. Christ's death, the ultimate act of obedience, gives God great honour. As it was beyond the call of duty for Christ, it is more honour than he was obliged to give. Christ's surplus can therefore repay our deficit. Hence Christ's death is substitutionary in this sense: he pays the honour instead of us. But that substitution is not penal; his death pays our honour not our penalty.[1]

Anselm said that if God were a mere man, he could just forgive someone without demanding payment, as he asks us to do. But because he is so infinitely great, sins against him are also infinitely great, and he cannot just forgive without receiving satisfaction. However, once God's honor has been satisfied, he is free to forgive our sins, which he does.

While Anselm was the first to fully develop the idea of Christ's death as a satisfaction paid to God, he was building on ideas that had developed in the church over many centuries. The Roman Catholic penitential system had developed over time. First, it was taught that a person had to do acts of penance to show his sorrow for sin. By going beyond what is required in

---

[1] *Theopedia*, s.v. "Satisfaction theory of the atonement," accessed March 17, 2020. https://www.theopedia.com/satisfaction-theory-of-the-atonement

meritorious acts, it is possible to earn an excess of merit. Christ was thought to have earned an excess of merit by his suffering and death, "and this is paid to God as a satisfaction or compensation."[1] With these concepts in place, a fully developed theory in which Christ makes a payment to God on our behalf and in which His merit applies to us is now possible.

This idea of the merit of one being applied to another is not limited to Christ in Roman Catholicism. In Medieval Roman Catholicism, if a person did more penance than is justifiably required, he could accrue excess merit. This merit can then be applied to another's sins. The Church claimed to have a treasury of indulgences consisting of the merits of Christ and the saints. This provided the rationale for the Medieval practice of selling indulgences, which were a way to buy pardon for sins.

It is here that we begin to see an essential difference in Classic-type views of the Atonement versus Satisfaction types. In the Classic Model, God's incarnation is necessary but *God is working in and through Christ* to accomplish the victory over the powers of evil. In Satisfaction-type views, the Atonement is made by *Christ as man in relation to God*, in other words, the essential thing is that a man needs to pay the honor or penalty.[2] This sets up a separation in the Godhead so that God can be seen as bringing wrath upon himself, or turning away from himself. For this to work, the divine and human must be separated to some degree so that God can "become sin(ful)." This is a challenge to the Tri-unity of God that is often overlooked.

Aulen said it this way: In the Classic Model, there is a "discontinuity in the legal order: there is no satisfaction of God's [penal] justice." Rather God's relationship to man is

---

[1] Aulen, 82.
[2] Aulen, 80-83.

viewed in terms of grace.

> In the Latin [satisfaction] type, the legal order is unbroken . . . in the payment of the required satisfaction . . . the continuity of the Divine operation is lost; for the satisfaction is offered by Christ as man.[1]

In other words, he is saying that you can keep the legal requirements intact, or the Divine operation intact, but not both. (We have not yet arrived at Penal Substitution in our overview. Anselm's theory views man's debt as a debt of *honor* to God. Penal Substitution says that man's debt is an unpaid *penalty*.)

The Moral Influence theory

Just a few decades after Anselm, Peter Abelard criticized his Satisfaction Model strongly, and promoted what has become known as the Subjective view, or Moral Influence theory of the Atonement. Quite simply, this theory says that the reason and need for the cross was as a demonstration of God's love. As we understand the depths of God's love for us as displayed by Jesus' death on the cross, our own hearts are awakened to love him in return, and by his example of loving self-sacrifice, we are changed. While this is no doubt true, and these ideas have always been around, many have found this explanation for the need of Jesus' death inadequate as a stand-alone theory. During the Middle Ages, it was preferred over Anselm's view, and even today is widespread,[2] and has tended to be the favorite idea of liberal theologians to the rejection of the other views.

---

[1] Aulen, 146.
[2] Driver, 46.

Penal Substitution

In the thirteenth century, Thomas Aquinas stated that our debt to God is one of punishment, not honor, as Anselm had said. With this distinction, Aquinas established the underpinnings of the modern understandings of Penal Substitution.

However, the way Aquinas formulated this reinforced the Roman Catholic penitential system, and could be interpreted as supporting good works as involved in salvation.[1] The Reformers did not like that, of course. Martin Luther, John Calvin,[2] and others nuanced the theory in different ways. There has never been complete unity in Protestantism on the doctrine of the Atonement, but the view popularized during the Reformation, and that prevails today, can be simply described as "Penal Substitution." Briefly stated, this is the idea that Christ saves us by taking our justly deserved punishment upon himself, thereby experiencing the wrath of God in our place. As a consequence, our debt to justice is paid, and we can go free.

Most of the 16th and 17th century Reformers followed this Penal Substitution Model of the Atonement. It became firmly entrenched in their thoughts, creeds, and confessions. For many, Penal Substitution is the gospel.

As an example, the Westminster Larger Catechism, question

---

[1] Aquinas believed that a man could make satisfaction for his sins by doing penance. However, doing penance could not make satisfaction for *original sin.* In his view, Jesus' death accomplished this. "Though original sin has less of the nature of sin than actual sin has, yet it is a more grievous evil, because it is an infection of human nature itself, so that, unlike actual sin, it could not be expiated by the satisfaction of a mere man." *Summa Theologica,* "Whether man can make satisfaction to God", https://www.ccel.org/ccel/aquinas/summa.XP_Q13_A1.html accessed August, 2020.

[2] In teaching that Jesus died to pay for the (actual) sins of the elect, Calvin avoided any suggestion that penance could make satisfaction for those sins, which Jesus had already paid for.

49, says this:

> Q: How did Christ humble himself in his death?
>
> A: Christ humbled himself in his death, in that having been betrayed by Judas . . . having also conflicted with the terrors of death, and the powers of darkness, *felt and borne the weight of God's wrath*, he laid down his life an offering for sin, enduring the shameful, painful, and cursed death of the cross.[1]

As another example, the Westminster Confession says,

> Christ, by his obedience and death, did fully discharge the debt of all those that are thus justified, and did make a proper, real, and full satisfaction to His Father's justice in their behalf.[2]

Other models

There have been quite a number of other Atonement models promoted in the past few centuries, and especially in recent times, such as the Governmental Model, the Acceptance Model, and the Scapegoat Model, but these are not important to the purpose of this writing, so we will not address them further.

Along the way, there have been notable evangelical theologians who have weighed Penal Substitution in the balances and found it wanting. A few would be Dr. John Lightfoot, Hugo Grotius, Paul Peter Waldenstrom, Gustav Aulen, and C.S. Lewis. There have also been groups such as

---

[1] "The Westminster Larger Catechism," A Puritan's Mind, accessed April, 2020, http://www.apuritansmind.com/westminster-standards/larger-catechism/ (emphasis added)
[2] *Westminster Confession*, Chap. XI. III.

the Evangelical Covenant Church who have rejected Penal Substitution.

In summary

That brings us to the present. Penal Substitution is the dominant view among evangelical Christians in our time and place. Those who emphasize the Atonement in terms of *Christus Victor* and *Recapitulation* see salvation as happening on a "battlefield" or in a "hospital." Those who adhere to Penal Substitution see man's problem with God as a *legal* one, with salvation happening in a "courtroom" where a legal answer is given to the problem that mankind finds itself in. From Anselm, to Aquinas, and on to the Reformers, the Atonement is described primarily in legal terms. In this worldview, "Law is the backbone, the framework, the granite foundation of the spiritual world."[1]

---

[1] This is Aulen's quotation of Emil Brunner. *Christus Victor*, 84.

PART 2

PENAL SUBSTITUTION REPLACED

CHAPTER 7

MAKING SENSE OUT OF THIS MESS

At this point, you may be thinking, "Does it have to be this complex? Isn't the gospel simple? Away with the theologians!" I don't blame you if you feel that way. Actually, I agree that we should be able to present the gospel in a simple fashion that everyone can understand and believe. But we have to admit that we have some handicaps. We don't live in the culture that the New Testament was written in, and sometimes customs and concepts that were obvious to them need to be explained to us. Sometimes the process of trying to understand their thought processes can make our heads hurt.

A good goal in theology should be for some people to spend a lot of time on tedious details so they can take things that may have appeared simple to people at one time and place, and make them simple again for people in another time and place.

As an example, for the Jews, the illustrations of the book of Hebrews correlated to memories of things they experienced. It would take little effort to form a mental picture of Jesus as a great High Priest. We, however, have to spend time and effort to imagine the kinds of things priests do and how they would relate to what Jesus has done. I, on the other hand, could tell you I flew in an airplane across the country and give you very little detail about how that worked. But someone from the Greco-Roman world would need a lot of explanation about how I lifted off the ground in a hunk of metal and traveled the distance from Jerusalem to Rome in a couple hours before they could make much sense of it.

One of the enticing things about Penal Substitution is that it is so simple. Some of this is due to the fact that it is a very simple one-step solution (Jesus takes our punishment) to a particular problem (we deserve punishment ourselves). Part of the reason, however, that it seems simple to us is that we are so familiar with the concepts involved (as mentioned earlier) that we don't spend time and effort thinking about whether they are logical. We simply assume that they are.

Unfortunately, I cannot replace the idea that "Jesus saves us by taking our punishment" with an equally simple phrase that gives a complete understanding of the Atonement.[1] The New Testament uses a number of images, or motifs, to give different pictures of what Christ did for us by his life, death and resurrection. The New Testament does not give a ten-point list explaining all that Christ did, and fitting all the points into one explanation. However, we can study the Scriptures and grow much in understanding what Christ did for us, and how he did it. We should be thrilled by the fact that we will never understand everything about the Atonement, and can keep learning and growing as long as we live!

Though Penal Substitution describes the problem and solution too simplistically, the gospel should be able to be described in simple terms. Jesus and the Apostles were able to boil it down

---

[1] The Scriptures do give a number of simple summaries of Christ's work, but these need a bit of explanation and fitting together. One such summary is Romans 14:9 "For to this end Christ died and rose and lived again, that He might be Lord of both the dead and the living."

to the phrase, "the gospel of the kingdom."

What is the "gospel of the kingdom?" The gospel of the kingdom is the good news that the King has come, overcome sin, death, and the devil, and that you can surrender to his Lordship and be part of his kingdom! This is a simple gospel message that all can understand. I propose that if you spend time thinking about Christ as Victor, setting us free from sin and death, that this will become natural to your thinking.

CHAPTER 8

WHY DID WE NEED SOME GOOD NEWS?

Jesus came proclaiming the good news (gospel) of the kingdom with the words, "Repent, for the kingdom of heaven is at hand."[1] What is the good news of the kingdom? Many say the gospel is the news that your sins can be forgiven and you can go to heaven. Certainly that is a part of it, but the statement that your sins are forgiven says nothing about a kingdom.

God spent thousands of years setting the stage for Jesus to arrive and bring in the kingdom of God. So to introduce the good news of the kingdom, some background of world history and God's unfolding plan will be helpful. However, for most of my readers, the story will be quite familiar, so please feel free to skip to chapter 10.

For those who are still with me, let's go through a brief summary of the events that happened that left the world in need of good news and a new kingdom.

God created a world that was "very good"[2] and then gave it to Man—Adam—to rule over. Shortly thereafter, Adam and his wife Eve sinned after listening to the tempter Satan, and the

---

[1] Matthew 3:2, 4:17, Mark 1:15, Luke 10:9
[2] Genesis 1:31

cosmos was plunged into ruin.[1] Because of sin, Adam died (first spiritually, eventually physically) as God had warned would happen.[2] God said, "Cursed is the ground for your sake."[3]

It is important to understand that God did this for man's good. How much greater depravity would man have sunk to if he had lived with his sinful nature in a perfect world that gave him no troubles to slow down his evil? We do not know, but we do know that God knows what is best for us. Thus, the creation was subjected to decay, and it is very obvious to the observer that things in this creation are falling apart and wearing out.

Adam was the head of the human race, and mankind was the appointed ruler of the earth.[4] Despite man's sin, God did not cancel this privilege.[5] But Adam passed down a spiritual inheritance to all of us that shows brokenness at its core. All his descendants have shown that they have a corruption, a tendency to sin, imprinted in them. And so all "have sinned and come short of the glory of God."[6]

Now at first, it may seem unfair that we would be affected by Adam's sin, but a little reflection shows that it is reasonable. If the father of a large family becomes a drunkard, his family suffers. It is the course of nature that they suffer the consequences of his sin. He has been appointed to provide for them. If he abdicates his responsibility, they go hungry. The only alternative would be if God specifically intervened every time someone sinned to stop the consequences of that sin. That might seem nice, but that would not be the course of nature. It would continually violate the laws of cause and effect. And

---

[1] Romans 8:20-21
[2] Genesis 2:17
[3] Genesis 3:17
[4] Genesis 1:26
[5] Psalm 115:16
[6] Romans 3:23

God would probably end up taking away man's free will in the process. So, if free moral agents commit sin, and God does not specifically intervene to undo it, the results are not his fault. It is only natural that what was corrupted in Adam's nature became our inheritance.

Actually, the good news is that God did get to work to solve the problem, but it would be thousands of years before the solution to man's sin would come "in the fullness of time."[1] But that's getting ahead of ourselves . . .

Mankind fell through listening to the devil rather than to God. Unwittingly, our foreparents came under the power of sin, death, and the devil. Man, who had been the ruler of the earth, came into bondage to Satan, and Satan became "the god of this age,"[2] the ruler of the kingdoms of this world.[3] God needed to do something to both fix the sin problem and restore his creation.

Within ten generations, mankind had become so corrupt that God decided to wipe the earth clean, with the exception of the only remaining righteous family. Noah and his family were saved from a flood that wiped out and reshaped the world. As Noah's family emerged from the ark, God gave a new commandment; "You shall not eat the flesh with its life, that is, its blood."[4] God showed at this time (and also later) that there is something special about blood.

God had wiped the earth clean, but man's sin problem remained. It took only a short time until mankind again rebelled against God. Rather than worship him, they invented false gods that suited themselves and their lusts better. Knowledge of the true God faded until there were very few

---

[1] Galatians 4:4
[2] 2 Corinthians 4:1
[3] 1 John 5:21
[4] Genesis 9:4

who knew anything about him, and even fewer who worshiped him. Mankind was very lost, very sinful, and very unwilling to seek and find God.

Centuries after the flood as the knowledge of the true God was fading fast, God began to raise up a group of people to preserve knowledge of the truth and carry forward God's plan for redemption. Back at the very beginning of time, God had promised Eve that she would have an offspring (seed) that would bruise (crush) the head of the serpent (Satan).[1] God gave a similar promise to a righteous man named Abraham, saying, "In your seed all nations of the earth shall be blessed."[2] Whether Abraham knew it or not, his seed that would bless all nations was the same seed referred to in the promise to Eve.

Four hundred years later, Abraham's descendants had grown to several million people. God made a covenant with them, that if they would follow him, they would be his special people.[3] Along with this covenant, he gave them a set of laws to keep. With the establishment of laws and government, what had been a big family clan became a nation, and under the direction of God, possessed the land of Canaan.

The new people group that God had created became known as the Jews. In the code of laws that God gave them, he showed that "the life of the flesh is in the blood,"[4] that blood is needed to cleanse away sin[5], and to save life. A whole system of ritual offering was introduced to deal with sin and bring cleansing.

Although people did not understand very well at the time, these offerings were not in themselves efficacious. Instead, they were intended to provide pictures of something that God was

---

[1] Genesis 3:16
[2] Genesis 22:18
[3] Exodus 19:1-7
[4] Leviticus 17:11
[5] Exodus 29:36, Leviticus 16:19, Leviticus 16:30, Leviticus 8:15, Hebrews 9:22

going to accomplish in the future. We call them types and shadows. Nevertheless, at that time (as now) God was looking for people who would demonstrate their faith and love for him by their obedience. So he was pleased when people obediently followed his laws, such as by sacrificing lambs, and he forgave their sins, even though the sacrifice of the lamb itself had no inherent redemptive value.[1] He wanted to teach them lessons through this—lessons that sin brings death, life needs to be sacrificed (given) for us to have life, and that blood washes away sin, etc.

Sadly, although the Jews had made solemn promises of fidelity to God, they broke them time and again, and served false gods. God had to bring discipline again and again in order to bring about their repentance. Eventually, he had them deported to the land of Babylon for seventy years.

During this time, God raised up prophets who, with increasing clarity, prophesied of great changes and something immensely important that was coming. A good king named David was given a promise that God would establish David's offspring to reign from his throne forever.[2]

A prophet named Daniel prophesied of a "stone" made without hands that would smash all the kingdoms of the world and take their place.[3]

A prophet named Isaiah prophesied that a virgin would conceive and bring forth a son called "God with us." [4]

A prophet named Jeremiah prophesied that the time was coming when God would replace the original covenant that he had made with the Jewish people with a "new covenant." This

---

[1] Psalm 50:12-15
[2] 2 Samuel 7:16
[3] Daniel 2:31-45
[4] Isaiah 7:14

new covenant contained wonderful promises![1] God would take away their sins, give the people a new heart, and everyone would know him personally, from the least of them to the greatest. People would not have to go through an earthly priest anymore to access God. One of the reasons God gave that he would bring in a new covenant was because of how badly they had broken the old one.[2] The old covenant had not proven to be a fix for man's sin and the terrible situation the human race had gotten itself into. The first covenant was becoming obsolete, and would be replaced by the new covenant.[3]

The Jews were thrilled with these prophecies, and looked forward to the man who would inaugurate them. This man was called the Messiah, and he was the hope of Israel. They eagerly awaited his coming.

At the same time, however, there were prophecies that were less understood and appreciated. These were prophecies of a servant of God who would suffer. He would be cruelly put to death. He would give himself for others, yet in doing so he would take away their sins. But it was hard to understand how these things could be, and the Jews focused more on a great leader who would deliver them from their oppressors.

By this time, mankind had a track record of thousands of years of failure, selfishness, misery, and rebellion. Knowledge of the true God was scarce, and men who were in an obedient relationship with him were even scarcer, and mostly confined to the Jewish people. Men committed unspeakable acts of barbarism toward each other, and group after group came to power and attempted to enslave and dominate other peoples. Most people worshiped idols of wood and stone with rituals of human sacrifice, prostitution, and every imaginable indecency.

---

[1] Jeremiah 31:31-34
[2] Jeremiah 31:32. Compare to Hosea 11:7
[3] Hebrews 8:13

It was clear that mankind was in great sin and darkness, unable to save themselves from themselves. They were enslaved under evil and merciless demonic powers that held the world in their grip.

The Jewish people themselves had come under servitude to the Roman Empire. In a time when being conquered by another kingdom was taken as a sign that the gods of the conquerors were stronger than the gods of the conquered, it certainly looked as if Jehovah's name and reputation were suffering. The Jews sighed and groaned and waited eagerly for the day when the long-awaited Messiah would burst on the scene. He would liberate them, and vindicate them before the world.

If ever the world needed the good news of God coming to set things right, it was now.

CHAPTER 9

THE GOOD NEWS ARRIVES

Jesus the Hero

It is natural for mankind to love stories of heroes. This is because we imagine ourselves in their place—wielding the sword, saving the city, riding out the storm. We can almost imagine the sweet taste of fame upon our lips or the applause of the spectators. In Christ's kingdom, however, we learn that true joy and satisfaction comes when we give all our glory to Him alone and hold none of it back for ourselves. He is the true Hero of every story. He is the true victor of the great battle. He is the one who showed us that true heroism is gained by taking on oneself the form of a servant. All praise and glory to Jehovah alone!

> *Not far off in the shadows,*
> *Neither of mythic size,*
> *But human, and scarred, stands Jesus*
> *With a love glow in His eyes.*

Not known as an expert marksman
Not noted for strength of limb,
Yet the voice that rang o'er the stormy sea
Still calls men unto Him.

He took on mortal weakness
That He might feel our pain.
He took the form of a servant,
And counted His loss as gain.

He gained our souls through suffering–
And what a terrible cost!
From death He emerged the victor,
To save to the uttermost.

The risen Lord, our Daysman
Sits at the Father's hand.
He has been given all power,
To heaven and earth command.

So let us be glad, and worship!
And follow the path He trod,
Through death to follow His leading,
That praise may abound to God!

In the fullness of time, the angel Gabriel visited a young virgin named Mary and told her that she would miraculously conceive a son, the Son of the Highest, and call him Jesus.[1] He would be the one through whom the ancient prophecies would be fulfilled, and he would reign on the throne of David.

An angel told Mary's fiancé, Joseph, that the child she would bear would be the one who "would save his people from their

---

[1] Luke 1:31, 32

sins."[1]

A priest named Zachariah prophesied that this child would be the means by which God would redeem his people and bring salvation to them, delivering them from their enemies.[2] His birth was accompanied by a proclamation of "on earth peace, goodwill toward men."[3] These statements were about deliverance, salvation, and mercies. These wonderful promises—the good news, or "gospel"—are focused on a king, a kingdom, a victory, and deliverance from oppression, affliction, and sin.

Jesus grew to manhood, modeling the righteousness with which all men should have lived. He was obedient to his earthly parents. Throughout his whole life, he never sinned once, although he was tested in every area like we are.[4] This testing and personal victory is necessary for the work of salvation that he did for us, as we shall see.

When he was about thirty years old, Jesus was called by his heavenly Father to begin an active spiritual ministry. He summed up his mission with these words, "I have come that they may have life, and that they may have it more abundantly."[5]

He expanded on this with a quote from Isaiah:

> The Spirit of the Lord is upon Me, Because He has anointed me to preach the good news to the poor, He has sent me to heal the brokenhearted, to proclaim liberty to the captives, and recovery of sight to the blind, to set at liberty those who are oppressed, to

---

[1] Matthew 1:21
[2] Luke 1:76-77
[3] Luke 2:14 KJV
[4] Hebrews 4:15
[5] John 10:10

proclaim the acceptable year of the Lord.[1]

But it took more than a simple proclamation to bring this complete salvation to pass. While Jesus was on earth, he was at war. To all outward appearances, he was a gentle and meek lamb. And he was. But spiritually, he was raiding and pillaging the forces of evil. He described this as binding the strongman, so that he could enter the strong man's house and spoil his goods.[2] The signs of his power and warfare consisted in the fact that he was casting out demons[3] and healing people. The demons crying out and coming out proved that they were being bested.[4] He used physical healing to prove that he was, in fact, also forgiving people's sins.[5] He used it to demonstrate that he was able to reverse the effects of the curse of Adam, and that this was a sure sign that the kingdom of heaven had arrived.

The war continued to grow in intensity, and eventually came to a head.[6] Jesus knew that the climax was coming. Only Jesus understood that the victory would be accomplished through his death.

The great battle happened this way: Satan overplayed his hand, and inspired wicked men to capture, condemn, and crucify Jesus, unaware that he was sealing his own doom.[7] There was a betrayal by one of Jesus' friends. There were a series of false trials in which Jesus was condemned on trumped up charges.[8] Jesus was beaten, mocked, whipped within an inch of his life, and finally crucified. The forces of evil gathered

---

[1] Isaiah 61:1, Luke 4:18
[2] Matthew 12:29
[3] Matthew 12:28
[4] Luke 11:20
[5] Matthew 9:5
[6] John 12:31
[7] C.f. 1 Corinthians 2:8, Ephesians 6:12, Colossians 2:15
[8] Matthew 26:59

on the rocky hillside of Jerusalem to leer and gape in their glee.

> Many bulls have surrounded Me; Strong bulls of Bashan have encircled Me. They gape at Me with their mouths.[1]

The spotless Lamb of God, pinned between heaven and earth, passed minute after minute of grueling agony. The sky grew dark as heaven and earth trembled at the awesome tragedy of God himself killed by his own creation. After hanging on the cross for six hours, his final moment came.

With a loud voice, Jesus cried, "It is finished," and the earth shook at his cry as he bowed his head and died. Through it all, he did not sin. He submitted to his Father's will. He trusted God. He forgave his tormentors. He showed love in every way. He endured righteous and faithful unto the end. Upon his death, he was hastily put in a tomb.

Something happened in the spiritual world. The prophecy to Eve had been that the serpent would bruise the heel of the promised Seed, and the Seed would crush the head of the serpent.[2] These actions can be seen as simultaneous. Jesus' heel was bruised as he stomped on that vile snake. But the snake was crushed! This happened, not through physical weapons, swords, and combat, but because of a spiritual principle that Paul expressed, "Do not be overcome of evil, but overcome evil with good."[3]

Jesus did the most righteous thing that has ever been done in his submission to death and suffering, and as a result, the serpent received his fatal blow.

---

[1] Psalm 22:12. I am uncertain whether "bulls of Bashan" here refers to people or demons, but I'm sure the demons were there gloating.
[2] Genesis 3:16
[3] Romans 12:21

(To apply this to ourselves, we need to understand that the *very act* of responding to evil by doing good is actually waging warfare in the spiritual realm. Returning good for evil involves suffering, but is actually an integral part of how we overcome Satan's stratagems. If someone strikes you on one cheek, and you strike back, the conflict spreads. Evil grows. However, if you absorb the evil by responding in love, you choke evil at the source.)[1]

Jesus, through his righteous suffering, was perfected. As such, he became the author of eternal salvation to all who obey him.[2] He gave his blood to wash away our sins. When our sins are washed away, the devil loses his power over us.[3]

Death swallowed Jesus, but death could not contain him. Three days later, accompanied by an earthquake and announced by a magnificent angel, Jesus rose from the grave! His soul did not remain in Hades, and his flesh was not allowed to see decay.[4] He appeared to the women who first came to his tomb, saying "Rejoice!" He appeared to his disciples, who had become a frightened, disoriented little band, with the kind words, "Peace be unto you." In this he showed them that he had forgiven them for their forsaking him in his hour of trial, and that his goodwill toward them was still the same.

After forty days of appearing to his disciples, he ascended back to heaven, disappearing in a cloud as he went. But he left them with a promise that someday he would return in glory, and meanwhile he would be present in and with his disciples by his Holy Spirit. In heaven, he was crowned as king and sat down at the right hand of the Father, where he ever lives to make intercession for his people. And because of this, he is able to

---

[1] Romans 12:17-21
[2] Hebrews 5:8-9
[3] Luke 11:22
[4] Acts 2:27

save to the uttermost those who come to God through him![1] As proof of his crowning and kingship, he poured out the Holy Spirit on the Day of Pentecost.[2]

As Jesus parted from his disciples, he instructed them, "Go and preach the good news to every creature."[3] So that is the task he has given to his people. It is now our task in the rest of this writing to more fully unpack what that good news is. We will try to answer the question of what it means that Jesus "died for our sins according to the Scriptures," and how that death brought our salvation.

It is my hope and prayer that this will be a journey of discovery for you, and that in the process, your awe and wonder of Jehovah will increase to more and ever more awe and wonder, worship and praise!

---

[1] Hebrews 7:25
[2] Acts 2:30-33, Philippians 2:5-8, Hebrews 2:5-8, Acts 17:7, Daniel 7:14, Zechariah 14:9
[3] Mark 16:15

CHAPTER 10

CHRIST THE VICTOR

Hallelujah, It Is Finished

Hallelujah! It is finished,
Let the valleys echo back,
Let the hills rebound the tenor of the song,
For the conqueror Death is vanquished
By the Victor on the rack.
Hallelujah to the One whom praise belongs.

How the Savior quelled the Serpent
With unfathomable rout!
While ten thousand, thousand angels stood in awe;
When He died by cruel torment on the dark and dreadful
mount—
Let this story every ransomed saint enthrall!

He has dealt in lovingkindness
Of His mercies I will sing
With my mouth His faithfulness will I make known.
I will lift my hands to heaven
In surrender to my King,
And will cast myself in rapture at His throne!

Hallelujah, hallelujah, to the Lamb that was slain,
Hallelujah, hallelujah is our joyous refrain.
Let us sing a song of praise!
Glory, glory to the Lamb
Hallelujah to the great I AM. Amen.

Is Penal Substitution (Jesus enduring the wrath of God in our place) the best explanation for how Christ saved us, or do the scriptures interpret Jesus death another way? To be fair, thoughtful exponents of Penal Substitution present it as a part of a much larger picture, and decry the tendency of many in their camp to focus almost entirely on the idea that Jesus bore the wrath of God so that we would not need to, while ignoring other facets of Christ's work.[1] Yet they still see this idea as the most important part of the Atonement.[2],[3]

Our task now is to look at what the Scriptures really teach about the cosmic problem, and what God did to fix it. In the last chapter, we looked at the historical sequence of the events of Jesus' life and ministry. In this chapter, we will focus more on the spiritual significance of the events.

Mankind's problem

Through the sin of one man, Adam, death entered the world. Because the whole human race was at that time *in him*, death spread to all men. This death is a spiritual death. The reason

---

[1] Jeremy Treat, *The Crucified King: Atonement and Kingdom in Biblical and Systematic Theology* (Grand Rapids, MI: Zondervan, 2014), 177-179.
[2] Treat, 193.
[3] J.I. Packer, "What Did the Cross Achieve: The Logic of Penal Substitution," *The Highway,* accessed November 24, 2019 http://www.the-highway.com/cross_Packer.html Packer says "I am one of those who believe that this notion takes us to the very heart of the Christian gospel."

that all men die this spiritual death is because each inherits the corrupted nature of Adam, and consequently sins.[1],[2] Our primary problem, then, is that we are sinners, spiritually dead, and therefore separated from God. We cannot resurrect ourselves. We cannot give ourselves life. We are unable to get ourselves out of this mess. We need someone who has life-giving power to come and infuse it into us.

At the same time, we have another very serious problem. We have a cunning enemy, the devil, who knows how to tempt us into sin, and thereby entrap us. This is how he got power over Adam and Eve. It is why he is said to have had the power of death. Part of our liberation from slavery to sin and resulting death needed to be the destruction (binding) of this devil, who had the power of death.[3] His dominion over sinful mankind is so total that it can be fairly said that "the whole world lies under the sway of the wicked one."[4]

People can even be divided into the children of God and the children of the devil.[5] Sin, death, and the devil are so tied together that John can say,

> For this purpose, the Son of God was manifested, that He might destroy the works of the devil [death and

---

[1] Romans 5:12-13
[2] An infant who dies a physical death as a result of conditions in this fallen, imperfect world does not have a chance to sin, and therefore does not die spiritually. Paul said in Romans 7:9, 11, "I was alive once without the law, ... for sin taking occasion by the commandment, deceived me, and by it killed me [spiritually]."
[3] Hebrews 2:14-15 says, "Inasmuch then as the children have partaken of flesh and blood, He Himself likewise shared in the same, *that through death He might destroy him who had the power of death*, that is the devil, and release those who through fear of death were all their lifetime subject to bondage." (emphasis added). The word for "destroy" can be translated as "to deprive of force, influence, power." (*Thayer's Lexicon*)
[4] 1 John 5:19
[5] 1 John 3:10

sin].[1]

The author of Hebrews says, "that through death He might destroy him who had the power of death, that is, the devil."[2]

We needed deliverance from sin, death, and the devil. Regarding deliverance from sin, it is worth noting here that Matthew says of Jesus, "He will save His people from their sins."[3]

This is quite different than saying that "He will save his people from the *punishment* for their sins." Our primary problem is *not* that we are headed for punishment. Our primary problem is that we needed our sins (and resulting separation from God) dealt with.

Regarding deliverance from death, God told Hosea, "I will ransom them from the power of the grave; I will redeem them from death."[4]

Regarding deliverance from the devil, we could refer to Isaiah 49:24, "Shall the prey be taken from the mighty, or the lawful captive delivered?"[5] Or to the words of our Lord, as recorded by John, "Now is the judgment of this world; now the ruler of this world will be cast out."[6]

Sin, death, and the devil are linked together in a kind of evil trinity, because it is the devil who inspired sin, it is sin that brings death, and it is the devil who has the power of death.[7] So to come under one of these three is to come under the power of all, but to be delivered from one of these is to be

---

[1] 1 John 3:8
[2] Hebrews 2:14
[3] Matthew 1:21
[4] Hosea 13:14
[5] KJV
[6] John 12:31
[7] 1 John 3:8, Romans 5:12, Hebrews 2:14

delivered from all. To be delivered from these is to be *given life!*

The Exodus story typifies man's bondage to Satan. Like the devil, Pharaoh would not let the children of Israel go. He wanted to keep them in bondage. But the Lord delivered them from his hand. In the prophets, it is repeatedly said that the Lord redeemed them (the Israelites) from Egypt. God even told Isaiah, "I gave Egypt for your ransom, Ethiopia and Seba in your place."[1]

Yet there was another, greater ransom/redemption that was needed and was prophesied. Jesus said that this one was drawing near with these words,

> For even the Son of Man did not come to be served, but to serve, and to give His life a ransom for many.[2]

God's problem

God is, and always has been, the King over all the earth.[3] But most of his subjects had rebelled. And even those who still desired to serve him had sinned, and thus had come under the power of death. God's kingdom needed to be re-established on earth.[4] Jesus came to recover what had been lost to the kingdom of God. But to do that, would obviously provoke a battle with the usurper, the devil. The devil would have to be dealt a decisive blow that would weaken him to where he could not put up enough resistance, and God's creation could

---

[1] Isaiah 43:3
[2] Mark 10:45
[3] Psalm 47:2
[4] I think it is correct to think of the Father as King until he sent Jesus. He is, of course, still over all (Ephesians 4:6), but he has committed the kingdom into the hands of his Son. See Psalm 2:6, Luke 19:12, 1 Corinthians 15:27 for example, and many other passages.

be restored.

Jesus' teachings

When Jesus burst onto the scene, he brought the good news, healing, and deliverance.[1] He spent three and a half years teaching people truths about God, and how God wanted them to live. Mankind had gotten far from understanding God's true nature and how to live lives pleasing to him.

Jesus came to bring life, but that life would have done little good if people kept on wallowing in their sins, and consequently bringing death back upon themselves. Similarly, teachings about how to live do little good unless they are accompanied by divine life, for without the enabling power of divine life working in us, we are unable to follow these teachings anyway.

God had a standard that he had never fully unveiled prior to Jesus, because he knew it was impossible (at that time) for people to follow. He had given them an inferior Law.[2] It told them what to do, but it did not carry the power to change the heart. And they found it impossible to keep even that law. So, when Jesus taught, he said a number of times, "You have heard that it was said by them of old—but I say unto you . . ."

Each time he explained the full righteousness of God, and raised the standard of righteousness from what they had understood from the Mosaic Law. Only through the strength and grace that Jesus gives us can we live up to his teachings. The Mosaic Law restrained the evil of man with its "eye for an eye and a tooth for a tooth"[3] teaching. It remained for Jesus to

---

[1] Luke 4:18-19
[2] The Mosaic Law. Hebrew 7:18-19 explains its inadequacies.
[3] Exodus 21:24

fully unveil the righteousness of God by saying,

> But I tell you not to resist an evil person. . . .
> But I say to you, love your enemies, bless those who curse you, do good to those who hate you, and pray for those who spitefully use you and persecute you.[1]

Jesus, in his life and ministry, demonstrated what God is really like. He modeled it in every way. He told us to be perfect, even as our Father in heaven is perfect.[2] He told us to forgive those who wrong us, because that is what the Father does.[3] And he did this himself, showing that he is one with the Father, and does whatever he sees his Father do.[4]

The goal of salvation is not simply to escape punishment, but to be restored to what God originally intended mankind to be, in relationship to him. We have to know how God intended for citizens of his kingdom to live, to thereby experience all the blessings of God and bring him glory. For this to happen, we need to have the teachings of Jesus, showing us how to live.[5]

Jesus' death

Then came the climax of Jesus' work on earth. He had predicted this event and its result when he said,

> Now is the judgment of this world; now the ruler of this world will be cast out. And I, if I am lifted up from the earth, will draw all peoples to Myself.[6]

---

[1] Matthew 5:39, 44.
[2] Matthew 5:48
[3] Matthew 6:12
[4] John 8:28, 12:49
[5] 1 John 2:6
[6] John 12:31-32

If we look for summary statements of how Jesus viewed his life and work, we find his words:

> For even the Son of Man did not come to be served, but to serve, and to give His life as a ransom for many.[1]

The apostle John gives two statements that provide a nice summary of Jesus' work:

> And you know that He was manifested to take away our sins,[2]

and

> For this purpose the Son of God was manifested, that He might destroy the works of the devil.[3]

The captives are about to be set free! The Son of Man was about to be lifted up on the cross, but for those who had spiritual eyes to see, it would not be Jesus who was receiving the death blow.

God's justice

In our culture, when we think of the word "justice," we tend to equate it with retributive justice (punishment). Because of this, when Penal Substitution tells us that God's justice had to be "satisfied," we assume this is saying that someone needs to be punished. However, in the Bible, the words translated "just" and "justice"[4] are the same as those translated as "righteous" and "righteousness." God's righteousness and his justice are the

---

[1] Mark 10:45
[2] 1 John 3:5
[3] 1 John 3:8
[4] Hebrew *tsaddiq, mishpat*; Greek *dikaios, dikaiosyne*

same thing.

To understand that this is so, we must realize that what these words have in common is their connection to what is "right"[1] and upright. For example, sometimes the right thing to do is to punish,[2] and giving "penal justice" is what is right. Other times, the right (*dikaios*) thing to do is to show mercy. In this case, showing mercy is the righteous and just thing to do! The righteous/just man is the one who acts in accordance with God's will, and this sometimes means showing mercy and other times giving judgment.[3]

We can see this in Matthew's account of Joseph.

> Then Joseph her husband, being a just man, and not wanting to make her a public example, was minded to put her away secretly.[4]

Because Joseph was a "just" (*dikaios*) man, he wanted to show mercy to Mary.

Matthew also records the parable of the landowner who promised his laborers, "You also go into the vineyard, and whatever is right I will give you."[5]

---

[1] Greek *dikaios*
[2] Lest I be misunderstood, Christians are called in this age to show mercy, not to punish others. However, this has to do with their calling to reveal God's grace to the world. The Lord has given the "sword" to the state. But in the church, we are not to wield authority as the Gentiles (Matthew 20:25). (Christians do exercise a measure of penal justice in their families when they discipline their children. However, this is to be corrective rather than vindictive, or even strictly retributive. However, that is outside the scope of this book.)
[3] The New Testament teaches us to give judgment, as in church discipline. We are called to be righteous/just as God is (1 John 3:7). However, this is distinct from vengeance, which God has reserved for himself (Romans 12:19). Only God knows how long to keep showing mercy, and how to give vengeance with perfect justice.
[4] Matthew 1:19
[5] Matthew 20:4

The landowner offered to give his laborers whatever is "right" (*dikaios*). In this case, he decided it was righteous/just to give those who had worked one hour the same as those who worked all day! This certainly looks like a case where justice is mercy.

When someone suffers wrongfully, the Father by nature of his righteousness/justice is obligated to right the wrong. But evidently, he is not obligated to right it immediately. We know that all wrongs done to us will be righted at the last judgment (if they have not been righted before). But God *may* right the wrong immediately. Vengeance belongs to God. Those who deserve vengeance have no right to a delay in receiving their just punishment. But because God is very merciful, he may delay a very long time before bringing vengeance.

God has more than one way to right wrongs. One way is to punish the wrongdoer. He is generally slow and reluctant to do this. Most of the criminal justice system today thinks that this is how to right wrongs. They lock people up, or put them to death. The justice that is brought to a situation by punishing the evildoer is called *retributive* (penal) justice.

Another option God has is to reward the wronged party. If someone steals my car, and God has limitless cars, out of his generosity, he can just give me a new one. He can even give me a much better one! Now, as far as I am concerned, justice has been done to me. I need wish for nothing more. I am no longer out of a car, and my needs are taken care of. God's *rewarding* or *restorative* justice has been called "*premial justice*." [1]

(We are required to believe by faith that God will operate this

---

[1] Ronald L. Roper, "Premial Justice, the Unjust Cross, and Power from on High [Complete Paper]," The Premial Atonement: accessed November 24, 2019. https://premialatonement.wordpress.com/premial-justice-the-unjust-cross-and-power-from-on-high/

way by the commandment to not demand our goods back if someone steals them.[1] Letting them go is a sign that we believe God will repay us.)

From God's perspective, however, justice has not yet been fully served because the car thief has not gotten what he deserves. The sin he has done has marred God's good creation, and remains unresolved. So at some point, God will repay the thief with tribulation.[2] But that is not the way God would prefer to demonstrate his righteousness. He prefers that the thief would repent. That would allow him to let the thief off the hook. To this end, he may withhold *penal* justice from being served to the thief for a while. If the thief would repent, then the right/just/righteous thing for God to do would be to forgive him and show mercy![3]

It is righteous of God to bring deserved punishment. It is righteous of him to bring deserved reward. The fact that God rewards those who suffer wrongfully with *premial* justice is a precious truth. When you suffer wrongfully, you earn the right to a reward![4]

Overcoming evil with good

When we suffer for God, we actually become accounted worthy of inheriting the Kingdom of God! At the same time, our persecutors become worthy of God's vengeance.[5] It is

---

[1] Luke 6:30
[2] Even this is a mercy if it brings the thief to repentance before his chances run out. God's predominant disposition is to show mercy. "... Mercy triumphs over judgment" (James 2:13).
[3] This is shown by 1 John 1:9. "If we confess our sins, He is faithful and just to forgive us our sins and to cleanse us from all unrighteousness." See Appendix B, 1 John 1:9.
[4] 2 Thessalonians 1:6-7, 2 Corinthians 4:17, 1 Peter 2:20, Romans 2:6, 7
[5] 2 Thessalonians 1:4-9

imperative that we understand that doing good is actually a form of warfare; it is actually how we overcome evil. As Paul instructed, "Do not be overcome by evil, but overcome evil with good."[1]

In the Bible, God is often pictured as a warrior. He wears armor; he rides on a white horse. He has a sharp sword going out of his mouth. We should understand that these are symbols given to us to relate to things we are familiar with. But they are no more literal, carnal weapons, than are the "weapons of our warfare" mentioned in 2 Corinthians 10:4 and described in Ephesians 6.[2]

According to Isaiah 59:17, God's breastplate is righteousness, his helmet is salvation, his cloak is zeal. his sword is not a piece of sharp steel clenched in his teeth—it is his Word.[3] God the Warrior does battle in righteousness and zeal, and with his Word.

Jesus went up and down the land doing warfare, drawing toward the climactic battle. He did warfare by doing good—praying, casting out demons, healing the sick, and teaching the truth.[4] As he did so, he was binding the strongman.[5]

He sent seventy disciples out to preach and to heal.

> Then the seventy returned with joy, saying, "Lord, even the demons are subject to us in Your name."[6]

Jesus replied, in my paraphrase,

> You saw people healed and demons leaving. But I saw

---

[1] Romans 12:21
[2] Isaiah 59:17
[3] C.f. Revelation 19:15 and Ephesians 6:17
[4] Acts 10:38
[5] Matthew 12:28-29. C.f. Luke 13:16.
[6] Luke 10:17

through and beyond that. I saw the shaking and
crumbling of Satan's kingdom. While you only saw the
physical visible side, I was seeing Satan fall from
heaven.

Satan had earlier gained power over humanity. He was the one who had the power of death. When man sinned and fell under the devil's power, God could not simply take away the devil's lawful captives, because the fact that they were under his power was due to their sins. The only way to set mankind free was to deal with the sin problem.

Satan was able to stand in the presence of God, before his throne, and accuse even the brethren day and night.[1] It seems Satan could not be cast out of heaven until that ability could be terminated.[2] The sin that put people under his power needed to be taken away.

God knows how to ensnare the wise in their own craftiness.[3] We can only speculate about what might have motivated Satan to inspire the killing of Jesus. Perhaps Satan thought that since he had the power of death, if he could kill the Son of God, he could keep him a prisoner. Perhaps he thought if he could remove Jesus from the world stage, Jesus would no longer be able to bring salvation. Maybe he thought that if he could cause Jesus enough pain and torture, he could get Jesus to sin and come under the devil's power as had the rest of humanity, and thereby lose his power of an endless life. Maybe in his lust and irrational evil, Satan simply could not stop at any point in bringing evil and misery. Who knows what he thought? But he played into the hand of God.

Thus, on the cross, Satan expended all his fury against Jesus. To the very end, Jesus showed how to respond to evil against

---

[1] Revelation 12:10
[2] See Romans 8:33-34
[3] Job 5:13

oneself. When reviled, he did not revile in return. When he suffered, he did not threaten, but committed himself to him who judges righteously.[1] He forgave his persecutors.

Something happened in the spirit world. An earthquake shock occurred that spread even to the physical world.[2] When Jesus had passed every needed test, and demonstrated every needed truth without wavering from righteousness, he cried out "IT IS FINISHED!" He bowed his head and gave up the spirit. At that moment, Satan had lost. I do not know if Satan knew immediately that he had been defeated. Perhaps he did. Perhaps he learned it when Jesus descended to Hades and announced victory. Perhaps he did not know until Sunday morning, when Jesus rose from the dead. It matters little. But that moment when Jesus cried, "It is finished!" the battle was over. Jesus had overcome evil with good.

Satan had lost all his armor in which he trusted.[3] Jesus, by being perfected through suffering, had become the Author of eternal salvation.[4] Jesus' blood had been shed, and was now available to wash away the sins of the world. With redemption available through the blood of Jesus, the sins of the past (and those in the future) could be fully dealt with.[5]

God now could cast Satan out[6] and chain him up, and Satan had no bargaining chips left. True, he wasn't willing to leave heaven. True, this required a battle up there, in which Michael

---

[1] See 1 Peter 2:23
[2] Matthew 21:51
[3] Luke 11:22
[4] Hebrews 5:8-9
[5] See Romans 3:25
[6] Luke 11:22, Mark 3:27 and Matthew 12:29 (c.f. also John 12:31 and Revelation 20:2) seem to indicate that Christ bound Satan at his first coming. It must be noted that this binding is partial. Satan cannot touch the Christian but he still holds sway over the world (1 John 5:18). Satan is tied with a long chain, so to speak. In Hebrews 2:14, Jesus is said to have destroyed the devil. However, the Greek word for "destroy" can be translated as "reduce to inactivity, or render powerless," and this is probably the intended meaning.

and his angels cast out Satan and his angels. The actual casting of Satan out of heaven to return no more does not seem to have happened until Jesus ascended back to be coronated.[1] But Satan had, by the arrival of evening time on Crucifixion Day, lost all his armor in which he had trusted.[2] He had no grounds on which to stay. Kicking and screaming,[3] he was hurled to the earth.

Resurrection

Jesus' body lay in the tomb. The Jewish leaders felt an uneasy triumph. He was dead, but such strange things had happened! Hadn't he said something about coming back after three days? What if his disciples tried to fake a resurrection? Better put some guards there! To the world it looked as if Jesus' movement was defeated. It looked as if all his promises of a coming kingdom had failed. It even looked as if God had punished him with the death of an impostor! Shaking their heads, the chief priests had said, "He trusted in God; let Him deliver Him now if He will have Him."[4]

But it did not look as if God had delivered him. Jesus was dead.

But then on the third day, Jesus rose from the dead! With an earthquake, an angel from heaven descended and rolled away the stone from the door. Jesus appeared to his disciples and proclaimed, "All authority has been given Me in heaven and on earth."[5]

---

[1] Revelation 12:5, 7; Daniel 7:13, 14
[2] Luke 11:22
[3] Metaphorically speaking!
[4] Matthew 27:43
[5] Matthew 28:18

Forty days later, Jesus ascended to heaven. But he ascended with a promise. He would send the Holy Spirit to dwell within his people and give them the power he had promised to continue with his mission until he comes back. Ten days later, on the day of Pentecost, he fulfilled this promise.

Premial justice in the Resurrection

God, in his mercy, would tarry nearly another forty years before bringing *penal* justice on the Jewish nation for the horrific murder of his Son. (He brought penal justice upon them in the destruction of Jerusalem.[1]) He would allow many to repent in the interval and thereby escape the coming penal justice altogether. But he *could not wait* to reward Jesus according to his *premial* justice! Jesus had been tortured and killed unjustly, and had responded with the greatest display of righteousness ever seen. Justice *required* a reversal of this unjust sentence. Justice required a resurrection!

> [Jesus] God raised up, having loosed the pains of death, because it was *not possible* that He should be held by it.[2]

Our just God delights in bringing justice to his people. When God dispenses a reward, it is "to give to everyone according to his work."[3] That seems to indicate that in some measure it is *proportional*.[4]

---

[1] Matthew 22:7
[2] Acts 2:24, emphasis added
[3] Revelation 22:12
[4] Another example of proportionality is in the parable where one man earns ten minas, and receives ten cities. Another man earns five minas, and is over five cities (see Luke 19:11-27). Five or ten cities is astronomically more reward than a five or ten-mina increase deserves, but it appears that a proportionality is maintained.

However, our generous God delights in rewarding with way more than is due. His rewarding, or *premial* justice is superabundant. In the Law, this principle is seen in the restitution a thief has to make. The thief is expected to restore four sheep for a sheep and five oxen for an ox.[1] Similarly, in the case of Job, God restored double everything Job had lost.[2]

As humans, we can understand God's desire to give a superabundant reward. If you were an elderly millionaire without an heir, and you saw a young man helping an old lady across the street, you might well say, "That's the man I want to leave my money to." Your fortune is not equivalent to his act, but you want to lavish what you have on someone. That is why Paul can say,

> For our light affliction, which is but for a moment, is working for us a far more exceeding and eternal weight of glory.[3]

In the case of Jesus' crucifixion, a great sin had been committed. But instead of recognizing that, people were saying that Jesus must have come under the judgment of God. God wanted to vindicate himself, and show his justice. He did so by raising Jesus from the dead. However, it was not enough to merely reverse the effects of crucifixion with a resurrection. He *lavished* power and glory on Jesus, and gave him a kingdom. God also gave him the "promise of the Father"—the Holy Spirit—with which to baptize his followers.[4] Then, because Jesus is so good, and so generous, he promptly shared these battle prizes with us. We too are now seated in heavenly places because we are in Christ Jesus.[5] And he poured out the Holy

---

[1] Exodus 22:1
[2] Job 42:10
[3] 2 Corinthians 4:17
[4] Acts 1:4, 5
[5] Ephesians 4:6

Spirit upon his followers.

Therefore He says:

> "When He ascended on high,
> He led captivity captive,
> And gave gifts to men."[1]

Resurrection life

As humans had lost their spiritual life through sin, they needed it restored. Jesus came to do this. He said, "I have come that they may have life, and that they may have it more abundantly."[2]

This is where the need for the blood of Jesus comes in, and why it is so important.

As mentioned before, God had made it clear that "the life of the flesh is in the blood."[3] The blood carries life-sustaining oxygen to the body's cells, and carries away their impurities. When blood flow stops, the body dies.

The elaborate sacrificial system that God had set up as part of the Jewish religion was designed to emphasize this truth. When men sin, they lose their life, which brings death upon themselves. Because of the death brought by sin, they need an infusion of life. When an innocent animal was slain, it was symbolically giving its life on behalf of the offerer. In the Law, there was no elaborate ritual for the animal's death. Its throat was simply to be slit. All the focus of the ritual was on what happens with the blood. It was the blood that was important.

---

[1] Ephesians 4:8
[2] John 10:10
[3] Leviticus 17:11

Sometimes the blood was offered on the altar.[1] Sometimes it was applied to the horns of the altar of incense.[2] Sometimes it was sprinkled on people.[3] Sometimes it was poured at the foot of the altar.[4]

Because we have been engrained with the viewpoint of Penal Substitution, we tend to think that the sacrificial animal was taking the punishment of the sinner. But the Jews did not think of it this way. Punishment of animals is not even hinted at in the Levitical law. The animal was giving its life—contained in its blood—to the needy offerer.

The thing that we need is life. Spiritual life is from the Spirit of God. He breathed it into Adam in the beginning. The Father has this life in himself, "and so he has granted to the Son to have life in himself."[5] Jesus can share this life with us.

> Most assuredly, I say to you, unless you eat the flesh of the Son of Man and drink His blood, you have no life in you.[6]

As I understand it, this blood is connected to his Spirit, which is where the life comes from.[7] The connection between blood and Spirit is so close that sometimes the terms are used interchangeably.[8] However, he had to literally give his flesh and blood on the cross, for this life (Spirit) to flow to us. There

---

[1] Deuteronomy 12:27
[2] Leviticus 4:7
[3] Exodus 24:8
[4] Leviticus 4:7
[5] John 5:26
[6] John 6:53
[7] Jesus mentions both flesh and blood. One way to understand this is as follows: his blood is connected to his Spirit. His flesh represents his human nature. He took our human flesh and glorified it. If we share in his nature, and thus his flesh, our flesh is redeemed from corruption also, and we will put on incorruptible flesh at the resurrection.
[8] Andrew Murray, *The Blood of the Cross* (New Kensington, PA: Whittaker House, 1981), 15.

is mystery here. The Bible does not tell us exactly why this is, or how it works, although we can make some guesses. We know something miraculous happened on our behalf as a result of Jesus' death. We know that Jesus was perfected through his sufferings. In some way, Jesus had to die and resurrect so that we could die and resurrect.

Identification with Jesus

We die and resurrect with Jesus by uniting with him. Adam is the old man—representing the old humanity.[1] Jesus, the new man, came to establish a "new humanity." To enter this new humanity, you have to "renounce your citizenship" in the old humanity. The old humanity (old man) is corrupted by sin and at enmity with God. Therefore, you have to crucify your old nature (old man) voluntarily. You have to die to your *self*.

When we die to ourselves, we identify with Jesus and share in his death. When we share in his death, we also become partakers in his resurrection. His resurrection life that the Father shared with him flows to us. We share in his life as his Spirit enters our mortal bodies, unites with our human spirit,[2] and gives spiritual life to us.

> God has given us eternal life, and this life is in His Son. He who has the Son has life; he who does not have the Son of God does not have life.[3]

This is what the "new birth" is all about. Your first birth was into a fallen race. In Adam, you die.[4] Being born again is about being born into a new family by the working of the Holy

---

[1] See Romans 5. C.f. Romans 6:6, 1 Corinthians 15:45, Colossians 3:9,
[2] 1 Corinthians 6:17
[3] 1 John 5:11, 12
[4] 1 Corinthians 15:22

Spirit. In your first birth, you came into the lost family of Adam. In your second birth, you come into the saved family of Jesus. That is why Jesus is called the "last Adam," or the "second Man."[1] He has restarted the human family as it was meant to be. To be born into his family is to be born anew.

His life enters us and cleanses (washes away) our sins. Because blood is used as a stand-in for life, the Scriptures often refer to the blood of Jesus that cleanses us from all sin. Just as blood carries away waste particles from the cells, so Jesus' blood/life flowing through us keeps us alive.[2] We still have a flesh/sin nature. This flesh keeps on producing junk. But as long as Jesus' blood keeps cleansing us, life keeps flowing through our "veins," keeping ahead of the death that is working in our flesh.[3] Our salvation is not just the bare fact that Christ died for us, but that it was only through his death that he could give his blood to bring us the important thing—life.

Death is conquered by life. "For the law of the Spirit of life in Christ Jesus has made me free from the law of sin and death."[4]

Ultimately, we still have to go through physical death. This is a great blessing, because the source of sin that is still in us as Christians resides in our body (in our flesh).[5] Originally, that sin also dwelt in our hearts. But when we surrendered to Jesus, we received a new heart, that is, our hard heart was transformed.

> Put on the new man which was created according to God, in true righteousness and holiness.[6]

---

[1] 1 Corinthians 15:45, 47
[2] Romans 8:10, 11
[3] 1 John 1:7-9
[4] Romans 8:2
[5] See Romans 7, especially verses 17-18.
[6] Ephesians 4:24, see Ezekiel 36:26

Our heart is now good,[1] but we are dragged downward by the sin that resides in our flesh. (We resist this downward pull by walking in the spirit. Paul says that if we walk in the spirit, we will not fulfill the lusts of the flesh.[2]) At physical death, our spirit, which has been transformed by Jesus' indwelling Spirit united with ours, is set free from the sinful prison of our flesh. Paul says, "O wretched man that I am! Who will deliver me from this body of death? I thank God—through Jesus Christ our Lord!"[3]

When we die, we leave behind the sin that dwells within us. God will resurrect us bodily later, and give us a new body, that has no sin nature and no death working in it; "then shall be brought to pass the saying that is written: 'Death is swallowed up in victory.'"[4]

This whole idea of Christ dying so that we could die may seem odd, if you have never heard it before. In *Mere Christianity*, C.S. Lewis tackles this topic, and here is how he presents it:

> We are told that Christ was killed for us, that His death has washed out our sins, and that by dying He disabled death itself. That is the formula. That is Christianity. That is what has to be believed. Any theories we build up as to how Christ's death did all this are, in my view, quite secondary: mere plans or diagrams to be left alone if they do not help us, and, even if they do help us, not to be confused with the thing itself. All the same, some of these theories are worth looking at. . . .
>
> When you teach a child writing, you hold its hand while it forms letters; that is, it forms letters because you are forming them. We love and reason because God

---

[1] Romans 7:21-22
[2] Galatians 5:16
[3] Romans 7:24-25
[4] 1 Corinthians 15:54

loves and reasons and holds our hand while we do it. Now if we had not fallen, that would all be plain sailing. But unfortunately we now need God's help in order to do something which God, in His own nature, never does at all—to surrender, to suffer, to submit, to die.[1] Nothing in God's nature corresponds to this process at all. So that the one road for which we now need God's leadership most of all is a road God, in His own nature, has never walked. God can only share what He has: this thing, in His own nature, He has not.

But supposing God became a man—suppose our human nature which can suffer and die was amalgamated with God's nature in one person—then that person could help us. He could surrender His will, and suffer and die, because He was man, and He could do it perfectly because He was God. You and I can go through this process only if God does it in us; but God can only do it if He becomes man. Our attempts at this dying will succeed only if we men share in God's dying, just as our thinking can succeed only because it is a drop out of the ocean of His intelligence: but we cannot share God's dying unless God dies; and He cannot die except by being a man. That is the sense in which He pays our debt, and suffers for us what He Himself need not suffer at all.[2]

Life through the blood of Christ

---

[1] David Bercot (via personal email from 11/23/17) points out that Lewis misunderstands the Trinity here, essentially equating Jesus with the Father. Because Jesus and the Father are different persons, Jesus is able to submit (and surrender) to the Father. However, Lewis is correct that suffering and death were not part of the experience of the Godhead until Jesus became human. So I believe Lewis's essential point is valid.
[2] C.S. Lewis, *Mere Christianity* (New York, NY: Harper Collins, 2001), 55, 56-57.

The Lord told Moses, "it is the blood that makes atonement for the soul."[1]

"Atonement" is here translated from the Hebrew word *kaphar*. *Kaphar* comes from the Hebrew root, *kpr*. Of this root, the *Theological Dictionary of the New Testament* says that we cannot decide between a meaning of "to cover" and "to wash away."[2] However, the context of many verses about atonement show a meaning of "to wash away" or "to cleanse."[3] For example, the Lord told Moses:

> For on that day the priest shall make atonement for you, to cleanse you, that you may be clean from all your sins before the Lord.[4]

Understanding that blood atonement in the Old Testament brought cleansing helps us see why the New Testament writers understood that Jesus' blood cleanses us, washing away our sins.

Under Penal Substitution, what is needed is Jesus' *sufferings*. The shedding of his blood is simply a by-product of the inflicted pain. However, the Bible tells us that Jesus' blood actually washes away our sins. He shed his blood so that it could do that. The Bible does not tell us *how* it does that. However, I will give you my thoughts about that in the next chapter.

---

[1] Leviticus 17:11
[2] *Theological Dictionary of the New Testament Vol. III*, 302.
[3] Perhaps there is a connection in that something must be covered with water to wash it. Blood covers our souls, washing them. Here are some verses that link atonement with cleansing: Leviticus 12:7, 8, 14:18-20; 14:31, 53, 15:13, 15, 30, 16:16, 19, 30.
[4] Leviticus 16:30

Defeat of Satan or cleansing from sin?

You may have noticed that two themes have been entwined throughout this chapter. One is the defeat of Satan. The other is our need to be given life through deliverance from sin. People have had a hard time keeping these ideas together. Some have emphasized our need for deliverance from the devil but in doing so have minimized our own bondage to sin. Others have focused almost entirely on man's sin problem and largely ignored the defeat of Satan.

I am not able to entirely fit these two themes together. Perhaps we don't need to. The writer of Hebrews is content in one chapter to state that Jesus suffered to bring many sons to glory, and that he died to destroy the devil.[1]

The writer doesn't explain if or how these two accomplishments are directly connected. However, I think the key may lie in the fact that his death led to his enthronement. It was after his resurrection that he said, "All authority has been given to Me in heaven and on earth." [2] Now that he is enthroned, he is able to reign in the midst of his enemies,[3] and send forth his Holy Spirit.[4]

Now, the Bible doesn't tell us whether Satan's actual capabilities were diminished through Jesus' death. When people drive out demons in the name of Jesus, and demons react violently to the mention of his name and his blood, something powerful is happening in the spiritual world that we do not fully understand. However, in parts of the world where the gospel has not penetrated, people seem just as bound in

---

[1] Hebrews 2:10, 14
[2] Matthew 28:18
[3] Psalm 110:1-2 The Lord said to my Lord, Sit at My right hand ... The Lord shall send the rod of Your strength out of Zion. Rule in the midst of your enemies!
[4] Acts 2:33

heathenism, superstition, and witchcraft, as they have been for millenia past. Until the gospel reaches them it does not appear that the devil's power over people has diminished.

The defeat and binding of Satan means that he cannot effectively resist the gospel. Jesus promised, "The gates of Hades shall not prevail against [the church]."[1] Twenty centuries of persecution have not stamped out the church. This demonstrates that Jesus is indeed sitting at the Father's right hand, ruling until his enemies are made his footstool.[2]

The overthrow of Satan is a glorious and exciting truth. But the thought that I am even more excited about is that Jesus' enthronement enabled him to pour out the Holy Spirit in a new way![3] Through the Holy Spirit, the blood of Jesus cleanses us from sin and we receive new life. Because we are empowered and cleansed, we can resist the devil on a personal level. With a new heart and a new Spirit[4] in us, the power of sin over us is broken. Satan cannot even touch the born-again Christian.[5] The life we receive through Jesus is something to really get excited about!

---

[1] Matthew 16:18
[2] Hebrews 10:12, 13; Acts 2:34, 35
[3] Acts 2:33
[4] Ezekiel 36:26
[5] 1 John 5:18. There is some debate about how this verse should be understood, but probably it should be understood as, "but he who has been born of God keeps himself [in the love of God], and the wicked one does not touch him [so long as he remains in the love of God].

CHAPTER 11

FURTHER THOUGHTS ABOUT THE ATONEMENT

It is only fair to begin this chapter with a bit of a disclaimer. Parts of this chapter constitute my own deduction about how the Atonement works, and may be incorrect. I offer it in hope that it is not far off the mark. If you find it helpful, may God be praised.

I have said that Penal Substitution is not in the Bible, but is rather a deduction, and an incorrect one at that. What does the Bible clearly say? The Bible tells us *that* the Atonement works, but it does not precisely tell us *how* it works. It tells us *that* Jesus' blood washes away our sins, but it doesn't tell us *how* Jesus' blood washes away our sins. The Bible tells us *that* the Spirit gives life, but it doesn't tell us *how* the Spirit gives life.

The Bible tells us that Jesus died *for*[1] (because of, on behalf of, as a response to) our sins—which is somewhat ambiguous. If Penal Substitution were correct, the Bible could easily have said that Jesus died to take the *punishment* for our sins. Or, to really make it clear, we could have been told that Jesus died to take our punishment—burning for burning, wound for wound, stripe for stripe. Instead, Isaiah tells us that "by His stripes we

---

[1] An example is Galatians 1:4, "gave himself for (*hyper*) our sins..." According to *Strong's, hyper* means "over, beyond, on behalf of, for the sake of, concerning".

are healed."[1]

It is as if we are to be content with knowing that we are healed, without knowing the mechanism by which his stripes heal us.

The fact that we are not clearly told *how* it works probably means one of two things: Either it is not possible for us to comprehend; or it is metaphysically difficult enough to comprehend that to explain the Atonement would be to put understanding it into the realm of the philosophers before whom the common man would have to grovel, admitting his ignorance.

We perceive the world through our five senses. But we cannot directly touch and taste spiritual realities. Thus, in the Bible, spiritual things are explained to us by relating them to physical things.

"A sower went out to sow his seed," said Jesus.[2] Think about it. The activity of a man scattering seeds on a plowed field bears little resemblance to a man standing on a street corner talking about Jesus.[3] But the picture of seed sown, growing, withering, and being harvested is a very effective way for us to understand spiritual realities.

Even in the physical world, there are things we cannot really grasp, because they are out of range of our five senses. For example, general relativity talks about the geometry of space. The math appears to work. But nobody really understands what curved space *really* is. So we are given examples from the three-dimensional world, and are told to visualize a rubber sheet, with heavy objects dimpling it. But this is only an analogy to help us understand effects. Four-dimensional space

---

[1] Isaiah 53:5
[2] Luke 8:5
[3] This is only an example comparison; preaching on a street corner is only one of a thousand ways to "sow seeds."

is not like three-dimensional space. Nobody can remotely understand what four-dimensional space "looks" like.

The Bible uses many images and metaphors to talk of spiritual things. Prophets have visions where kingdoms are viewed as beasts, or as parts of a statue. A river flows out of the threshold of the temple, and the farther it goes, the deeper it gets. We know that the beast that rises out of the sea is not a literal beast, but we are sometimes at a loss to know when things in heaven as described in the book of Revelation are literal or figurative. When the bride of Christ is pictured as a city, the New Jerusalem descending out of heaven, we scratch our heads. Perhaps a picture is being painted for us to grasp that there is untold beauty and pleasure there, and we can long for it.

Ezekiel sees a vision which he tries to describe for us; and we shake our heads in bewilderment. The living creatures run back and forth, in appearance like lightning. Beside each living creature is a wheel. In fact, it is like a wheel in the middle of a wheel. And what do you know, wherever the spirit wants to go the wheels go, because the spirit is in the wheel! The more Ezekiel tries to tell us about what he saw, the more confused we become. Perhaps we are to understand that spiritual things cannot be described well in physical terms.

Perhaps the Atonement is a bit like that. If God were to tell us how Jesus' blood washes away our sins, and how the Spirit gives us life, we might shake our heads in bewilderment. At the least, we would get hung up on trying to understand, and lose focus on what Jesus really wants us to grasp, which is to *love* and *be* and *do*.

When a person is saved from his sins—is washed by Jesus—he cannot say how it works. But he can feel that it has. (There is generally a sense of change, forgiveness, relief, when the Holy Spirit saves a person. However, we will not put God in a box. Someone might surrender to Jesus and feel little or no "warm fuzzy feelings."[1] Salvation is demonstrated by fruit, not feelings.)

My understanding of how the Atonement works

How does the Atonement save us? Having spent much time thinking about the Atonement and wondering where the clues lead, I would say that the ancient ideas of Recapitulation are getting close to the truth. Because we were alienated from God, and cut off from divine Life, Jesus had to take on a human body to unite the human and divine back together in the Incarnation. But this was not enough. He had to live and die and overcome testing in order to overcome sin in the flesh. According to Hebrews 2:10, this is how he was perfected. Having been perfected, he can share that perfection with us.

It is because he was (and is) a man that we are able to share in that perfection. We can share in a steak dinner because steak is basically what we are made of. We can take it into us, and be strengthened by it. We cannot share in a dinner of molten lead, because it is alien to our nature. Jesus' sharing in our nature made unity with God possible in a new way.

In the Bible, Israel is referred to as a unit. In fact, because of their solidarity, the entire people group was referred to as a man. God told Moses to tell Pharaoh, "Thus says the Lord: 'Israel is My son, My firstborn.'"[2] In Isaiah chapter one, the nation of Israel is a sick man:

> From the sole of the foot even to the head,
> There is no soundness in it,

---

[1] Josh McDowell is a good example. He writes, "After I prayed, nothing happened. I mean *nothing*. . . . In fact, after I made that decision, I felt worse. I actually felt I was about to vomit. *Oh no, what have I gotten sucked into now?* I wondered. . . . The change was not immediate, but it was real. In six to eighteen months, . . . My life *was* changed." [Josh McDowell, *More Than a Carpenter* (Tyndale House Publishers, 2009), pp. 161-162]
[2] Exodus 4:22

> But wounds and bruises and putrefying sores;[1]

This solidarity meant that the state of the nation affected everyone. Even though there were righteous people in Israel, they typically suffered right along with the unrighteous when God brought punishment. Godly Daniel was carried off to Babylon with everyone else.

This concept of Israel as a unit helps us understand why when Achan took the accursed thing, a curse came upon the whole nation. God said, "Israel has sinned, and they have also transgressed My covenant."[2] Only those who *participated* in Achan's sin (Achan's family) were *punished* for the sin, but thirty-six men died as a *consequence* of Achan's sin. God was not punishing those thirty-six men, but his protection over Israel was withdrawn, and they died as a result.

Our Western individualism has lost or neglected the corporate nature of life. We put our own needs and wants first, above those of society. (Divorce [and remarriage] is a great example. Those who pursue it think it is only affecting themselves, and do not realize how their actions affect society as a whole. The societal implications are one reason God has put such a strong prohibition on divorce and remarriage. Those who are divorced and remain single in obedience to God can derive some meaningfulness out of the fact that they are suffering for the good of society.)

In the Bible, the family of Adam is a unit; "as in Adam all die."[3] It might not seem fair, but it is inescapable. However, Jesus started the new family. If it is the case that all who are "in Adam" share in his death, then certainly, all who come into the family of the New Adam, share in the life of the New Adam.

---

[1] Isaiah 1:6
[2] Joshua 7:11
[3] 1 Corinthians 15:22

The Church in the New Testament is referred to as a unit. That is why the "body" image is used. Christ is the Head. We are the members.

When one member suffers, all suffer, says Paul.[1] "[As] all the members of that one body, being many are one body, so also is Christ."[2] According to this verse, Christ is not now merely the Man, Jesus, but is Jesus and the members of his body, the Church.

Man and woman become "one flesh."[3] This is not just a metaphor.[4] "One flesh" is a description of a reality.

> ". . . the two shall become one flesh." This is a *great mystery, but I speak concerning Christ and the church.*[5]

In a very real way, Jesus' blood washes us because we become *part of him*. "For we are members of His body, of His flesh and of His bones."[6] His blood is clean. Anything it touches cannot help but be washed clean. Because we are in solidarity with Jesus, his qualities are given to us through his Spirit. Through his Spirit, he transforms us.[7]

How are we part of Jesus? One way (if not *the* way) that we are part of him is by the fact that his Spirit is joined to our spirit. Like a man and woman become one flesh, he that is joined to the Lord is "one spirit."[8] The New Testament points to the fact that this is a deep and abiding reality—not just a metaphor. You become dead to the law *through the body* of Christ. In other

---

[1] 1 Corinthians 12:26
[2] 1 Corinthians 12:12
[3] Genesis 2:24, Mark 10:8
[4] A metaphor describes one thing in terms of another—i.e. a "wolf in sheep's clothing" is a metaphor for a false teacher. Of course, a false teacher is not a wolf in sheep's clothing in a literal sense, but is described that way.
[5] Ephesians 5:31, 32, emphasis added
[6] Ephesian 5:30
[7] 2 Corinthians 3:18
[8] 1 Corinthians 6:17

words, it is because he superseded the law that you can also be free from it—by being part of him.

> For the law of the Spirit of life in Christ Jesus has made me free from the law of sin and death. . . . But if the Spirit of Him who raised Jesus from the dead dwells in you, He . . . will also give life to your mortal bodies through His Spirit who dwells in you. . . . you received the Spirit of adoption.[1]

Since we cannot see the blood of Jesus fall on us at conversion, we must assume that the blood is something spiritual that is applied to our souls. Since our eyes cannot see spiritual things, and we cannot see souls, we cannot see the blood doing its work. But we know it does, because the Scriptures tell us so (and because our lives are changed). But how does Jesus' shed physical blood become spiritual blood? How does visible blood become invisible blood?

In the Old Testament, it is blood that makes atonement (cleansing) for the soul. Apparently, it can do this because it contains life[2]. If in the Old Testament, the blood of animals was used to purify (cleanse) the flesh, "how much more shall the blood of Christ . . . cleanse your conscience from dead works to serve the living God?"[3]

If the life of Jesus' flesh is in his blood, and his blood cleanses us, then the cleansing must occur when his life comes into us. And this life comes into us when his Spirit comes into us. Hence, the blood cleanses us through his Spirit coming into us.

> And there are three that bear witness on earth: the Spirit, the water [of baptism], and the blood [of Jesus];

---

[1] Romans 8:2, 11, 15
[2] Leviticus 17:11
[3] Hebrews 9:13, 14

and these three agree as one [for our cleansing].[1]

Unregenerate man has a kind of life that gives life to his soul and body. But it is not *eternal life*. Eternal life is a property of God. Only God has immortality[2]. In fact, the Scriptures nowhere teach that man was created immortal. His physical life was to be maintained by eating of the Tree of Life, which is how God planned to share his immortality in the Garden, and how he plans to share it in the New Jerusalem.[3] The Tree of Life may represent Jesus.

When man was cut off from God through sin, he was cut off from eternal life. That day, he underwent spiritual death, as he was separated from the eternal life that is in God, and his soul was corrupted. Man continues to have his spirit, with its temporary kind of physical life. In this, there is no visible difference between the Christian and the non-Christian. Both get old, decrepit, and die. But the Christian has his spirit joined in a "one spirit" union with Jesus, and this gives his spirit eternal life.

When a person dies, his soul and his spirit separates from his body. The body goes to the ground. But where does the spirit go? According to Ecclesiastes 12:7 (assuming this poem is giving didactic information), it returns to God who gave it. The non-Christian has lost his life. "But the rest of the dead [non-Christians] did not live again until the thousand years were finished . . ."[4]

When the Christian dies, the case is different. He has temporarily lost his body, but his soul lives (on), and reigns

---

[1] 1 John 5:8
[2] 1 Timothy 6:16
[3] Revelation 22:2
[4] Revelation 20:5 I am not addressing whether the unrighteous dead retain consciousness while they await the judgment. Whatever the answer to that, they have lost the quality that is referred to as "life."

with Christ.[1] Apparently, his soul remains alive, which would imply remaining connected to his spirit. How is this possible? Well, if his spirit is connected to Christ's Spirit, the mystery is solved. If I tie myself to my wife, wherever she is, there I will be: "your life is hidden with Christ in God."[2]

If my life/spirit is joined to Christ's Spirit, I could not lose my life unless he lost his. The soul of the Christian goes to be with Jesus.[3] The soul will be reunited with the body at the resurrection, and will spend eternity drinking and eating from Jesus, which I take as a metaphor for sharing in his divine life.[4]

It appears that the Holy Spirit could not come in this fresh, new, and promised way unless Jesus went back to heaven.[5] "Why?" you ask. According to John 7:39, the Holy Spirit was not yet given because Jesus was not yet glorified.[6] So Jesus was glorified when he ascended back to heaven, and that made it possible for his Spirit to be poured out on the day of Pentecost.

The disciples saw him and touched him after his resurrection. But after his glorification, he was so changed that the very glimpse of him blinded Paul, and John on Patmos fell at his feet as one dead. We do not know what happened in his glorification, except obviously, that he became more glorious.[7] But it seems obvious that the resurrected man, Jesus, on earth could not live inside people. When he went to heaven and was glorified, something was changed that made it so that his Holy

---

[1] Revelation 20:4 This is during the Millennium, which I understand to be a symbol for the church age. The Christian lives on and reigns with Christ after physical death.
[2] Colossians 3:3
[3] 2 Corinthians 5:8
[4] Luke 22:14-18. By saying this is a metaphor, I am not discussing whether we receive life through partaking of communion bread and wine. That is outside my scope here.
[5] John 16:7
[6] Compare to Acts 2:33 and 3:13
[7] This probably involved restoring the glory that he had laid aside when he became incarnate, as is described in Philippians 2:6-7.

Spirit could come to live inside of each and every Christian, far and wide on the planet.

Jesus called this giving of the Holy Spirit the "promise of the Father." But who was the promise to? To us, no doubt, but to us *through Jesus.* The Holy Spirit proceeds from the Father.[1] But the Holy Spirit comes to us *through Jesus.*[2] At the risk of speaking foolishly about things that are too high for us, think about it as a transformer. The 14,000 volts flowing in the powerlines past my house would be worthless to me without a transformer. If I tried to connect to them, I would be blown to bits. But a transformer takes 14,000 volts and connects it to my house in the form of a very usable 120 volts. We were unable to be united to God until Jesus the God-Man became the Mediator—the Transformer in our analogy.

Jesus, the glorified Man, who rose again with human flesh is in the bosom of the Father. Because of this miracle of the Incarnation, our humanity can be united to him, and his divinity is united to the Father. In Jesus' words to his Father, he prayed,

> You Father, are in Me, and I in You; that they also may be one in Us, . . .[3]
>
> I in them, and You in Me; that they may be made perfect in one.[4]

And thus, through Jesus, we are united to the Father.

Now, I have talked a lot about the Incarnation, and how it affects us. This has been referred to as our "divinization". Have we lost sight of the death of Jesus? The question deserves to be

---

[1] John 15:26
[2] Acts 2:33
[3] John 17:21
[4] John 17:23

asked: "How does the death of Jesus fit into this picture?" As we think about all these things, we must keep coming back to the suffering death of Jesus. Historically, Christians taught that Jesus' ministry spanned his life on earth and continues in heaven, but his suffering and death is the centerpiece of that drama. As the Nicene Creed says:

> For us men and for our salvation he came down from heaven: by the power of the Holy Spirit he was born of the Virgin Mary and became man. For our sake *he was crucified* under Pontius Pilate; *he suffered, died, and was buried.* On the third day he rose again in fulfillment of the Scriptures; he ascended into heaven and is seated at the right hand of the Father. He will come again in glory to judge the living and the dead, and his kingdom will have no end.[1]

By becoming a man, he could die. By dying a cruel death, he condemned (overcame) sin in the flesh.[2] In dying, he disarmed death itself. We needed these things done, but we could not do them ourselves. Only one who was perfect could suffer on behalf of sin, and overcome sin. So, *in a very real sense, he took the consequences of our sin, in his own body on the tree.*

This sounds SCARILY CLOSE to PENAL SUBSTITUTION! But there is an enormous difference! The difference is whether or not God the Father was pouring out wrath on Jesus because his nature forbids forgiving sin without punishment. And the answer, I believe with all my heart, is "No". But our sins meant that to save us, Jesus had to die. We participate in that death, overcoming of sin, and resurrection life which he won for us, by uniting with him. As a sacrifice, he did for us what we could not do for ourselves. And God in his righteousness repaid Jesus richly, reversing the unjust death, raising him up to be King,

---

[1] Nicene Creed, AD 325, emphasis added.
[2] Romans 8:3

and glorifying him. *Jesus is the hero!*

And where on this vast sea of ideas, pictures, and explanations are we left, clinging to our little dinghy? We can say with Paul:

> I am crucified with Christ; nevertheless, I live. Yet not I, but Christ lives in me: and the life which I now live in the flesh I live by the faithfulness of the Son of God, who loved me, and gave himself for me![1]

Well, there you have it. I gave what explanation I could. No doubt, there is far more to grasp and understand than I have yet apprehended. However, if you want to more fully understand the Atonement, this is the direction I think you need to push. But can you see the beauty and wisdom of the Scriptures in not telling us exactly how it works? Can you imagine the problems that would be caused if Christianity became an intellectual exercise, and you were thought to be a substandard Christian unless you could clearly articulate how Jesus' death saves you? Can you imagine the difficulty in taking the explanations of the previous thirty paragraphs to naked pagans, trying to convince those who have no background in philosophy and logic of how the Atonement works? Would it not hinder the gospel if we felt we had to explain the workings of the Atonement to those who don't yet even have theological categories in their minds?

God is wise. He told us that Jesus came to save us. He suffered for us. His blood washes away our sins. He gives us new life. Let us take this message to the world.

---

[1] Galatians 2:20, altered from KJV

CHAPTER 12

LIFE!

Faithful love flowing down from the thorn-covered crown,
Makes me whole, saves my soul,
Washes whiter than snow.
Faithful love calms each fear, reaches down, dries each tear;
Holds my hand when I can't stand on my own.

Faithful love from above
Came to earth to show the Father's love.
And I'll never be the same
For I've seen faithful love face to face,
And Jesus is His name![1]

Pulling it all together

At this point, maybe you are thinking, "That was long and complicated. I'd rather stick with a simple Penal Substitution." Well, let's see if we can boil this down a bit into something manageable:

We humans were dead in trespasses and sins, and in bondage

---

[1] Ken Young. "Faithful Love." © *Copyright 1993 by Hallal Music, used by permission.*

to the devil. We needed our sins washed away. We needed a heart change toward God. We needed new life.

Jesus, the Way, the Truth, and the Life had that life, and came to share it with us. To put the life of God in us required that God and man be joined. Jesus was incarnated, and united God's nature and human nature in a body of physical flesh.

Jesus taught us the ways of God so that we could become the kind of people God always intended us to be. God planned to sanctify and cleanse and empower people so that they could walk in his ways, and fellowship with him, but to walk in his ways requires knowledge of them.

On the cross, evil did its worst against Jesus. This was the climax of Jesus' life, his hour of greatest trial; yet he endured it without sin. Evil did not overcome him; by refusing to sin in response, he overcame evil. He condemned sin in the flesh.[1] He was able to offer himself without spot to God.[2]

Jesus learned obedience, and was perfected by his sufferings.[3] Because he conquered as he was tested, he is able to aid mankind in their testings. He poured out his life blood until he died. He tasted death for everyone.[4]

Through his death, he bound the devil. The devil had the power of death. Jesus conquered death, thus taking away the power of the devil. Because he was the Resurrection and the Life, and because he did not sin, death was unable to hold him.

In the Incarnation, Jesus united the divine to the human in his own body. Then, he took that body through death, by means

---

[1] Romans 8:3
[2] Hebrews 9:13-14
[3] Hebrews 5:8
[4] Hebrews 2:9

of the cross. Death could not hold him, and he overcame it in the resurrection. Because he rose from the grave, he ever lives above. He is able to share his life with anyone who wishes to receive it.

God the Father honored Jesus, the mighty Hero, and crowned him as King. He gave him power and glory, and set all things under his feet.[1] He continues to reign until the last enemy is destroyed.[2]

To receive the life that Jesus gives, you must first share in his death. That means laying down your own will in repentance, and accepting his will. You visibly participate in his death in baptism.[3] Jesus' blood washes away your sin. With your sins washed away, the devil loses his grip on you.

When you repent and lay down your own will, you clear the way for his Holy Spirit, the Spirit of Jesus, to enter you. It is this Spirit that gives you life. Your spirit is joined to his Spirit.[4] God's Holy Spirit of life dwells in us and purifies us. The Spirit, the water, and the blood agree in one.[5]

You come into the Body of Christ. This joins you to all other followers of Jesus who are also a part of his Body. As a member of his Body, you share in his power, life, and destiny. Jesus promised, "In the world you will have tribulation; but be of good cheer, I have overcome the world."[6] You will overcome through him.

In some way that is never fully explained in the Bible, when Jesus shed his blood, it enabled our sins to be washed away. It made it possible for our souls to be purified. It made it possible

---

[1] 1 Corinthians 15:27, Ephesians 1:22
[2] 1 Corinthians 15:26
[3] Romans 6:4
[4] 1 Corinthians 6:17
[5] 1 John 5:8
[6] John 16:33

for his Holy Spirit to come into us and be united with our spirit. Probably, it is through the union of God's Spirit to man's in the body of Jesus, and the subsequent way that Jesus was perfected through his suffering and death. Jesus' blood washing away our sins and the Spirit of Life coming into us are probably one and the same. At the very least, they are inextricably tied together. His blood keeps cleansing us as we walk in the light.[1]

We were reconciled to God by the death of his Son. When we see his love expressed to us through Jesus, our hearts melt. We were his enemies, but he melted our hearts, and we came to him asking for terms of peace[2] (reconciliation). When we united with him in his death, we gave up that part of ourselves that was at enmity with God. It is only because Jesus has already died that we are able to die with him. Now that we have been reconciled, we can be saved by his life![3]

Jesus was delivered over (to death) because of our offenses.[4] It was because of our sins that he had to die, and give up his life so that he could share it with us. This is how to understand "that Christ died for our sins according to the Scriptures."[5] He was raised again for our justification.[6] Jesus is the King! Because of his resurrection and resulting life flowing to us, we can be made just! As we unite with him, we share in his life and can receive every spiritual blessing he offers, along with the promise of a wonderful eternal future in a new heavens and a new earth.

This is the gospel, the good news of the Kingdom!

---

[1] 1 John 1:7
[2] Luke 14:32
[3] Romans 5:10
[4] Romans 4:25, altered from the KJV.
[5] 1 Corinthians 15:3; In other words, Jesus died because of, or on behalf of, our sins.
[6] Romans 4:25 KJV

But you don't even need to explain all of that summary to share the gospel with someone. You need to tell them that Jesus is King, that they must repent of their rebellion, trust in him, follow (obey) him, and he will cleanse their sins. If they heed the call to follow, Jesus will work out the rest.

This story of a sinless Lamb of God, who meekly, willingly laid down his life on behalf of humanity, seems to have a power all of its own to change hearts of stone. We do not have to understand how the Atonement works for it to work in us. As people look upon Jesus and behold a crucified, disfigured, bruised, and bloody man—as they hear that he did this for them—the Holy Spirit moves in their hearts. As people respond with,

> My Jesus, I love Thee,
> I know Thou art mine,
> For Thee all the follies
> Of sin I resign,[1]

the Kingdom of God relentlessly, inexorably, unstoppably, advances forward.

And this is the greatest story ever told!

---

[1] William R. Featherston, 1864

Conclusion

We have only scratched the surface of the subject of the Atonement. I set out on this writing because I realized that although there are many good books on the Atonement, they are mostly written by theologians to theologians. As much as possible, I have tried to avoid this trap.

I have attempted to shed light on the question of what it means "that Christ died for our sins according to the Scriptures,"[1] and how that death brought us life. As this writing has intended to show, the best way to understand this is that Christ died on behalf of our sins, because of our sins, or as a response to our sins. These are all acceptable ways to understand the phrase "for our sins." I have attempted to show that an alternative understanding, "Christ died to take the punishment for our sins" is not viable.

My goal has been as nearly as possible to discover what the Scriptures teach. While the concepts I have promoted are quite similar to what the early church believed, I have not attempted to prove that I am defending the early church view. This is because it is evident that their views are a bit of a spectrum, and also because they, no doubt, had not plumbed all the depths of what can be understood about Christ's work. And

---

[1] 1 Corinthians 15:3

neither have I.

> Oh, the depth of the riches both of the wisdom and knowledge of God! How unsearchable are His judgments and His ways past finding out![1]

I hope to learn and understand many more things about the Atonement as long as I live.

It is a tragedy that the greatest saga of all time has been so shrouded by theological argument and terminology that its majesty and mystery is often missed. In the Bible, we have the story of how God's world revolted against him, and how God in his great mercy did the impossible. He put himself in our shoes, to win us back, reclaim his creation, and undo all the evil that had been done. God invaded the universe in the form of a man, a man who allowed himself to be led as a lamb to the slaughter, and as a dumb sheep to the shearers.[2] All alone on a ghastly hillside, he grappled with the forces of darkness, and to their utter surprise, he came out victorious!

The saga continues today. For those who have eyes to see it, Jesus is the King, but the whole world still lies under the sway of the wicked one. There are many captives that need to be rescued. There is ground in our own lives that needs to be won. For those who want to share in the story, there is opportunity for selfless sacrifice, for deeds of daring, and for plundering the strongman's house. As we assault the gates of Hades, they cannot withstand our invasion, because the weapons of our warfare are not carnal,[3] and they are his weapons which he has put in our hands.

With joy we anticipate the day when the story is finished. Then, all will be summed up in him, and every knee shall bow,

---
[1] Romans 11:33
[2] Isaiah 53:7
[3] 2 Corinthians 10:4

and every tongue shall confess that Jesus Christ is Lord to the glory of God the Father.[1] And through and through, it is his work, and his story, and we delight in giving him the honor and glory which belongs to him.

As I think of this story, I cannot help but think of the words of Francis Thompson, who captured the battle for the souls of men in memorable verse:[2]

The Veteran of Heaven

> O Captain of the wars, whence won Ye so great scars?
> In what fight did Ye smite, and what manner was the
>   foe?
> Was it on a day of rout they compassed Thee about,
> Or gat Ye these adornings when Ye wrought their
>   overthrow?
>
> "'Twas on a day of rout they girded Me about,
> They wounded all My brow, and they smote Me
>   through the side:
> My hand held no sword when I met their armèd horde,
> And the conqueror fell down, and the Conquered
>   bruised his pride."
>
> What is this, unheard before, that the Unarmed makes
>   war,
> And the Slain hath the gain, and the Victor hath the
>   rout?
> What wars, then, are these, and what the enemies,
> Strange Chief, with the scars of Thy conquest trenched
>   about?

---

[1] Philippians 2:10-11
[2] Francis Thompson, "The Veteran of Heaven," *Masterpieces of Religious Verse*, 669. (Harper and Brothers Publishers, New York, 1948), 669.

>   'The Prince I drave forth held the Mount of the North,
>   Girt with the guards of flame that roll round the pole.
>   I drave him with My wars from all his fortress-stars,
>   And the sea of death divided that My march might
>   strike its goal.
>
>   What is Thy Name? Oh, show!—"My Name ye may not
>   know;
>   'Tis a going forth with banners, and a baring of much
>   swords:
>   But My titles that are high, are they not upon My thigh?
>   'King of Kings!' are the words, 'Lord of Lords!'
>   It is written 'King of Kings, Lord of Lords.'"

And I close with the words that are sung in heaven:

> Great and marvelous are Your works,
> Lord God Almighty!
> Just and true are Your ways,
> O King of the saints!
>
> Who shall not fear you, O Lord, and glorify Your
> name?
> For You alone are holy.
> For all nations shall come and worship before You,
> For Your judgments have been manifested.[1]
>
> You are worthy to take the scroll,
> And to open its seals;
> For You were slain,
> And have redeemed us to God by Your blood Out of
> every tribe and tongue and people and nation,
> And have made us kings and priests to our God;

---

[1] Revelation 15:3, 4

And we shall reign on the earth.[1]

Worthy is the Lamb who was slain
To receive power and riches and wisdom,
And strength and honor and glory and blessing!

Blessing and honor and glory and power
Be to Him who sits on the throne,
And to the Lamb, forever and ever![2]

Amen!

---

[1] Revelation 5:9, 10
[2] Revelation 5:12, 13

ADDENDUM

A WORD ABOUT WRATH AND RIGHTEOUS JUDGMENT

In this book, we have discussed that Jesus came to bring life,[1] and his first advent on earth was to declare peace on earth, goodwill toward men.[2] He did not do this by manifesting that God's wrath must be satisfied by punishing someone. Rather, he did this by walking among us and showing God's ways, and climactically, by humbly submitting to death at the hands of wicked men. He forgave them and did not revile, or retaliate. He did this "to give the light of the knowledge of the glory of God in the face of Jesus Christ."[3]

He called us to walk on earth, as he walked on earth. But does God punish, and bring penal judgment on sinners? The Scriptures clearly reveal that he does. "'Vengeance is Mine, I will repay,' says the Lord."[4] Jesus also came to warn. He warned about the results of sin and rebellion. He warned about what would happen to those who reject his offer of peace and goodwill. He warned that he would return in judgment. The apostles also warned of judgment to come as they gave the

---

[1] John 10:10
[2] Luke 2:14
[3] 2 Corinthians 4:6
[4] Romans 12:19

gospel message.

I have tried to show in this book that God loves mercy. However, we live in a time in which any mention of the wrath and righteous judgment of God is unpopular. I have a concern that my words not be used to minimize the fact that there is a coming revelation of the wrath and righteous judgment of God. That is why I add this section.

God desires that all men be saved and come to the knowledge of the truth.[1] But he has created men with the ability to decide whether or not they will surrender to him, and follow him. The Scriptures show that even now the wrath of God is revealed against those who reject him. When people reject him, he releases them to follow their own lusts into increasing darkness. Allowing them to go to the depths of depravity and lose reason and natural affection—in other words, turning them over to the consequences of their sin—reveals his anger against them.[2] People who refuse God's gracious gift of eternal life will stand naked in the judgment, unclothed by immortality. There, they will hear the sentence of the wrath and righteous judgment of God.

> Depart from Me, you cursed, into the everlasting fire prepared for the devil and his angels.[3]

God is unimaginably pure, good, and holy. He hates sin, which mars his creation and the souls who were made in his image. God allows men free will, with which they can choose to exercise evil during their lives on earth. He is able to use even man's evil to bring about good and to perfect those who are seeking glory and honor and immortality,[4] yet he hates the evil they do. He hates the evil they become. He plans to bring a

---

[1] 1 Timothy 2:4
[2] Romans 1
[3] Matthew 25:41
[4] Romans 2:7

final end to evil when he restores all things.

God is love. Love offers love, but does not force love upon someone. God offers people love, eternal life, relationship with him, and all the riches of his grace. But the only way to receive this love is to forsake one's sins. Sadly, many people love their sins, and prefer them to the offer of God's love.

God has ways of putting pressure on people. "He does not afflict willingly, nor grieve the children of men."[1] Yet he does allow or bring pain and troubles upon people in an effort to bring them to repentance, and to purify those who have already repented. But, if people choose to reject him, at the end of the day, God lets them do it.

God has a final solution to the problem of evil in the world. Those who persist in rejection of him will be cast into the lake of fire.[2] Nothing good will be destroyed, but only that which is irredeemable.

The righteous will rejoice that God has redeemed the world.

There will be no more pain nor sorrow. There will be no more curse, but his servants shall serve him. There shall be no night in the city of the saints, for the Lord God gives them light. And they shall reign for ever and ever.[3]

---

[1] Lamentations 3:33
[2] Matthew 10:28, Revelation 20:15
[3] Paraphrase of Revelation 22:3-5

APPENDIX A

WORDS ABOUT WORDS

As we study what the Bible teaches about the Atonement, we need to realize that some of the hard work has been done for us by translators. We rarely think about this as we read the Bible, but people have spent many thousands of hours discussing which are the best words or phrases to translate specific Greek words or concepts. In some cases, theologians have already done the hard and complicated work for us as they attempted to give us a simple Bible in language all can understand.

However, many of the translations we use were translated by people of certain theological persuasions. As hard as they may have tried to avoid it, in some cases their theology may have affected how they translated. The King James Version, for example, was translated by Anglicans and Puritans who believed in Penal Substitution. This may have affected words they used in a few cases.

Theology has a way of taking common words and giving them religious meanings. For example, "bishop," "deacon," "church," and "baptize" now have specialized religious meanings. But in Greek, the words that were used—"overseer," "servant," "assembly," and "immerse"—were simply everyday words that were used as needed to talk about things related to

Christianity. In Atonement theology, we have a similar situation with a few words. Penal Substitution has so dominated the way people think about Christ's death that some words have drifted from their original meanings.

To understand the Atonement, we have to understand the words that are used to speak about it. Some words have been given connotations from the Penal Theory itself. When words are understood in a certain way, it is difficult to see other possible meanings. In this section, we will look at word meanings and try to demonstrate their Biblical meanings.

Several of the words used in discussing the Atonement were coined by William Tyndale or brought into common usage by his English translation of the New Testament. He gave us the terms "mercy seat" and "scapegoat", and popularized the use of the word "atonement".

Atonement

> [W]e also joy in God through our Lord Jesus Christ, by whom we have now received the atonement.[1]

Tyndale probably did not actually coin the word "atonement". But he saw it as a meaningful way to translate a Greek word that means "reconciliation." "Atonement" is a compilation of "at", "one", and "ment." Literally, "at-one-ment" means to restore parties back into unity, or to change from enmity to friendship.[2]

However, in common usage, "atonement" now primarily

---

[1] Romans 5:11 KJV
[2] David Rolf Seely, "William Tyndale and the Language of At-One-Ment," Religious Studies Center, accessed April, 2020.
https://rsc.byu.edu/archived/king-james-bible-and-restoration/3-william-tyndale-and-language-one-ment

means "reparation for a wrong or injury." In other words, to make a payment to atone for wrong. This is a shift in meaning that has happened because of *theological* (Penal Substitution) perceptions of how Jesus brought atonement. Because Jesus is thought to have *paid* for our sins, when someone is said to "make atonement," the meaning is usually that he is making some kind of payment for what he did wrong.

Justice and Righteousness

We discussed justice at some length in Chapter 10, and discovered that "justice" and "righteousness" are used to translate the same Greek and Hebrew words. If reading Hebrew or Greek, we would not see the distinction that English makes between these words.

In our speech today, we generally use the word "just" in a context of someone handing out a punishment that is fair. If we say someone is just, we are usually saying they handed down an appropriate penalty. We are using the word to describe *penal* justice.

In the KJV New Testament, *dikaios* is translated as "righteous" forty-one times and as "just" thirty-one times. When the translators see the context is about criminal justice, the translators tend to translate the Hebrew and Greek words as "just" or "justice." When talking about social matters, they translate it as "righteous," or "righteousness." This is not wrong—it's just that we don't have a word in English that fully captures both aspects that are part of the Biblical words *dikaios, dikaiosyne, tsaddiq,* etc.

In the New Testament, justice/righteousness (*dikaiosyne*) usually refers to the "right conduct of man which follows the will of God and is pleasing to Him, for rectitude of life before

God."[1] This broadens the concept of justice far beyond penal justice, and includes a rewarding sort of justice. In other words, if I deserve a reward, you are being *just* if you give it to me and *unjust* if you withhold it from me. As mentioned earlier, this sort of justice has been referred to as premial justice. "Premial" means "rewarding" so "premial justice" describes God's actions when he rewards the righteous. Realizing that "righteousness" is synonymous with "justice" in biblical usage helps us to see that God displays his *justice* by rewarding the righteous. This is particularly evident in Psalms.[2] Here are two examples:

> Who may ascend into the hill of the Lord?
> or who shall stand in his holy place?
> He who has clean hands and a pure heart . . .
> He shall receive blessing from the Lord,
> And *justice* from the God of his salvation.[3]

> Deliver me in Your *justice*, and cause me to escape.[4]

Again, it is not wrong to translate "righteousness" here but then we lose sight of the fact that God's justice is *rewarding* as well as punitive. God's "righteousness/justice" is rewarding, gracious, merciful, and punitive as the case requires. In short, God loves whatever is upright.

Mary's husband Joseph showed that he was a just man by being kind![5] Herod feared John because he knew "he was a

---

[1] *Theological Dictionary of the New Testament, Vol. II.* S.v. "dikaiosyne." 198.
[2] Ronald Roper, "Appendix: God's Premial Justice in the Psalms," The Premial Atonement, accessed April, 2020,
https://premialatonement.wordpress.com/appendix-gods-premial-justice-in-the-psalms/
[3] Psalm 24:3-5, modified
[4] Psalm 71:2, modified
[5] Matthew 1:19

just and holy man".[1] Simeon was "just and devout."[2] "Cornelius [was] a just man, one who fears God."[3] These passages are not saying that these men were known for handing out judgments, but that they were upright.

Penal Substitution, by focusing on penal justice, has defined God's justice in terms of requiring punishment, and de-emphasized that God would prefer to be known for his goodness, kindness, and wonderful works to the children of men.[4]

Luther redefines justice/righteousness

To review what is stated in Chapter 5:

Martin Luther labored under guilt and inability to find peace with God. He had an epiphany however, and described his revelation in his exposition of Galatians 2:16.

> A wonderful new definition of righteousness! This is usually described thus: "Righteousness is a virtue which renders to each man according to his due. . . ." But here it says: "Righteousness is faith in Jesus Christ!"[5]

In other words, Luther is saying that righteousness no longer refers to being righteous, but instead refers to having faith in Jesus. Now, if a person has true saving faith, they will be counted righteous by God. However, with his distinction between active and passive righteousness, Luther separated obedience to God from faith in God. Faith became a mental

---

[1] Mark 6:20
[2] Luke 2:25
[3] Acts 10:22
[4] Psalm 107:31; see also Psalm 89:1 and Isaiah 63:7
[5] Alister E. McGrath: *Luther's Theology of the Cross,* 112.

assent to certain beliefs.¹ This allows a person to be considered to have faith even if their life does not show fruits of it. Martin Luther was trying hard to separate faith from any deeds of righteousness. (End of quote from Chapter 5)

We are saved by God's grace, and that grace is received through faith. It is obvious in the gospels that Jesus is looking for faith. "Believe on the Lord Jesus, and you will be saved . . ."² Paul speaks of human faith in Christ in Ephesians 1:15, Colossians 1:4, and 2:5. However, the way the Reformers interpreted some of the passages about faith, and then used that interpretation to set up a false dichotomy between faith and works has had dire results, leading many people to believe they are in a saving relationship with Jesus while actively living in sin.

Propitiation/Mercy Seat

The word "propitiation" occurs several times in the KJV. This is translated from the Greek words *hilasterion* or *hilasmos*.

In light of the vast quantities of ink that have been spilled in discussing the meanings of these words, it will be difficult to do them justice here. Nevertheless, I will try to bring some clarity on the subject.

---

[1] Martin Luther may not agree that his articulation of faith allowed for licentiousness. However, this seemed lost on his hearers, as it is demonstrable the Protestant Reformation caused an increase in immorality. For example, he wrote to a friend, "Be a sinner and sin boldly, but believe and rejoice in Christ even more boldly." Debates rage about this statement. Luther has his defenders who explain that he is misunderstood and quoted out of context. But Luther clearly believed something that caused him to make a statement that neither Jesus nor the Apostles would ever have said.
[2] Acts 16:31

Ancient Hebrew used a root *kpr* which had a root meaning of either "to cover" or "to wash away".[1] From this root we get the verb *kaphar*, which is translated a variety of ways. The KJV most commonly translates it "make an atonement" or "make atonement." It is also translated "purge," "purge away," and "cleansed" (among others). Sometimes, the context indicates that the purpose of *kaphar* is cleansing, as in Numbers 8:21: "Aaron made atonement for them to cleanse them."

When *kaphar* was translated in the Greek Septuagint, it usually became *(ex)hilaskomai*, and sometimes *katharizo*. *Hilaskomai* means:

> (mid.) to make atonement for, with a focus on the means for accomplishing forgiveness, resulting in reconciliation; (pass.) to have mercy on, be merciful to[2]

Hilaskomai appears in Hebrews 2:17 "make reconciliation for [or, have mercy on] the sins of the people"[3] and in Luke 18:13 "God, be merciful to me a sinner!"

Katharizo means "to cleanse." We see that the words *kaphar* was translated into are connected, although carrying different senses.

I have given these words and their meanings to give context for words that are related to them: *kapporet, hilasterion,* and *hilasmos*. We will see that these words include concepts of atonement, cleansing, mercy, and (protective) covering.

From the Hebrew root *kpr*, we also get the word *kapporet*. *Kapporet* probably means something like "protective covering"

---

[1] *Theological Dictionary of the New Testament [TDNT], Vol. III*, p. 302 says: "We . . . [cannot] make a definitive distinction between 'to cover' and 'to wash away.'"
[2] *The Strongest Strong's Exhaustive Concordance of the Bible,* Zondervan, 2001, p. 1505, *Strong's #2433.*
[3] Hebrews 2:17, KJV

(it may also mean "thing of cleansing").[1] This is the term for the covering that was placed over the Ark of the Covenant. It was not a part of the Ark, but was a piece of furniture in its own right, placed directly above the Ark.[2] According to Exodus 30:6, it was even more important than the Ark.[3]

The *kapporet* had two cherubim of gold, one on either end of it. These faced one another, and stretched out their wings over the *kapporet*. The reason for this is that God said he would speak to Moses from between the cherubim. So they were facing the spot from which God would speak to Moses. On the annual Day of Atonement, the high priest would take blood into the Holy of Holies and sprinkle it on the *kapporet*. The reason for this is probably that the blood was being brought as close as possible to God, who was seen as dwelling (in a certain sense) in the space just above the *kapporet*, between the cherubim. There, on the *kapporet*, atonement was made.

When the Septuagint was translated, *kapporet* became the Greek *hilasterion*. *Hilasterion* "can mean a means or place of expiation [atonement]."[4] It is also used simply to refer to the covering over the Ark of the Covenant, the *kapporet*.

When William Tyndale translated the New Testament, he chose the term "mercy seat" to translate *kapporet* and *hilasterion*. In the rest of this section, "mercy seat" will refer to the object in the tabernacle that was called the *hilasterion* or the *kapporet*.

Hilasterion and a related word *hilasmos* are translated

---

[1] Though *kapporet* is probably derived from *kaphar*, which is often considered to mean cover, the literal meaning of *kaphar* is wipe out, implying that *kapporet* means thing of wiping out / thing of cleansing--from Seraia Lexicon, s.v. "Kapporet," accessessed 12/2/19,
http://www.seraia.com/seraiauk/lexicon/Kapporet.htm
[2] *Theological Dictionary of the New Testament, [TDNT] Vol. III* p. 319
[3] *TDNT III*, 319.
[4] *TDNT III*, 319.

variously as "propitiation," "expiation," and "mercy seat." Before we go further, let's define "propitiation" and "expiation."

> **propitiate:** to gain or regain the favor or goodwill of : APPEASE[1]

> **expiate: 1 a:** to make amends for; **b:** to extinguish the guilt incurred by; **2** *obsolete:* to put an end to[2]

In Romans 3:25, Paul uses the word *hilasterion*: "whom God set forth as a *hilasterion* by His blood".[3] This is rendered "propitiation" in many versions, and "expiation" in others. Lots of debate has swirled around this word and this passage, and we will not be able to settle it here. But I will make a few observations.

Penal Substitution interprets this passage as saying that God propitiated himself (his own wrath) by the death of Jesus. But this is reading it backwards! The message of this verse is saying that God set forth Jesus as a *hilasterion*. A propitiation is offered by one person to appease another. If *hilasterion* means "propitiation" here, the verse would be saying that God offered Jesus to propitiate (appease) us!

In normal usage of the word "propitiation," one person does something to appease another. In Romans 3:25, God is the one setting Jesus forth as a *hilasterion* (propitiation?). It would then be a very strange concept to say that God is propitiating

---

[1] Merriam-Webster.com Dictionary, Merriam-Webster, s.v. "Propitiate" https://www.merriam-webster.com/dictionary/propitiate. Accessed April 16, 2020.
[2] Merriam-Webster.com Dictionary, s.v. "expiate"
[3] Romans 3:25

himself.[1]

Could *hilasterion* mean "propitiation"? The question is, did Paul use this word in the secular Greek sense, or did he use it as it is used in the Septuagint? The evidence points to the answer that he used it in the way it is used in the Septuagint. Paul quoted much from the Septuagint. It certainly formed his thinking. It seems quite unlikely that he would have used a familiar biblical word in an obscure and secular way. He would know this would cause confusion in his readers.

Thus, Paul certainly has the mercy seat in mind when he uses *hilasterion*. The question remains as to whether he is specifically saying that God set forth Jesus as a *mercy seat* or as a means of *expiation*.[2] In other words, is Paul saying that Jesus is the typological fulfillment of the mercy seat, or that he is the means of expiating (putting an end to, extinguishing, cleansing) our sins? Actually it makes very little difference. The mercy seat is the physical location where sins are dealt with. The cleansing away of sins is *expiation*. To distinguish between these two in Romans 3:25 would be to ask the question, "Is Jesus the place where our sins are dealt with, or is he the means by which our sins are dealt with?" Of course, he is both.

Many notable scholars have felt that *hilasterion* in Romans 3:25 is best translated as "mercy seat." Among these are the Greek Fathers (such as Origen), William Tyndale, Martin Luther, T. W. Manson, S. Lyonnet, A. Nygren, F. F. Bruce, J. N. Darby,

---

[1] *Hilasterion* is used in some classical Greek writings with a meaning of "propitiation." The question is whether Paul is using it in the Septuagint way or the secular Greek way.

[2] Some translations use the word "expiation." This is used to show that the action of *hilasterion* is directed toward us (propitiation is directed toward appeasing God). "In short, propitiation is directed towards the offended person, whereas expiation is concerned with nullifying the offensive act" (*New International Dictionary of New Testament Theology, Vol. III, p. 151* s.v. "Reconciliation," Colin Brown, ed.).

E. K. Simpson, W. D. Davies, and N. T. Wright.[1] If "mercy seat" is the best translation, Paul would be hearkening back to the Old Testament imagery of the mercy seat as the place where atonement is made, and saying that God is setting forth Jesus as the new "mercy seat," or place where we can find cleansing and reconciliation with God.

In 1 John 2:2, the word often translated as "propitiation" is *hilasmos*. A form of this word, *exhilasmos* is used in 1 Chronicles 28:11 (Septuagint) to mean "the place of the mercy seat." *Hilasmos* is rare in ancient secular Greek writings. However, it is used for appeasing the gods and expiation in general. In the Greek Septuagint, however, "God is not the object of *hilasmos;* the objects are rather people or their sins. . . . In Psalm 130:4, *hilasmos* is God's forgiveness." [2]

So when 1 John 2:2 says, "He Himself is the *hilasmos* [propitiation?] for our sins", it does not appear from the context that John is saying, "He is the past sacrifice by which God was appeased." Rather, the thought is that "he himself (his person and ongoing ministry—not the past event of his death) is currently the means by which our sins are forgiven and cleansed."[3] "Expiation" is a good translation here in 1 John 2:2.

Ransom

As mentioned earlier, the idea of Christ's death as a ransom loomed large in the minds of some, to the point that they saw it as the most essential thing about the Atonement, and speculated that Christ's death was in some way a ransom

---

[1] Driver, 237. Wright, 306.
[2] Driver, 153. In other words, in the Old Testament, *hilasmos* is not something directed toward God. Rather, it is directed toward (dealing with) people or their sins.
[3] 1 John 1:9 supplies the context for Jesus' dealings with our sins in 2:2.

payment to the devil. While this is possible, it is clear that the word "ransom" and the corresponding term "redeem" are used metaphorically in Scripture. ("Ransom" is a noun for the payment price. "Redeem" is a verb describing the action of ransoming.)

For example, God says in Micah 6:4,

> For I brought you up from the land of Egypt,
> I redeemed you from the house of bondage.

Redemption ordinarily requires a monetary price to buy a slave back from slavery. But clearly, no one in Egypt received a payment from the Lord as he bought his people back. At least not a payment they wanted! The usage is metaphorical. God says in Isaiah 43:3, "I gave Egypt for your ransom." There was no payment to Pharaoh, who represents the devil—this is metaphorical.

In Hosea 13:14, God says,

> I will ransom them from the power of the grave;
> I will redeem [purchase] them from death.

Thus, it seems reasonable that the New Testament could simply be using "redeem" and "ransom" metaphorically to describe the fact that we were in bondage, and the Lord delivered us from it.

1 Timothy 2:6 states that Jesus "gave Himself a ransom for all". "For all" means "on behalf of all", not "in place of all". The idea is not that he gave himself as a ransom price to God to take our punishment (as taught by Penal Substitution), but rather to save us when we couldn't save ourselves. The ransom price was the cost of his life, which is what it took to save us. The usage is metaphorical. Nobody got "paid".

Certainly, it is possible to imagine ways in which Jesus paid his life as a ransom price to the devil to set us free. If that helps you, it will do no harm to think of it that way. The one thing that I think will not work is to imagine that Christ bought us *from* God *to* God. Acts 20:28 refers to the "church of God, which He purchased with His own blood." If the Father already owned it, why did Christ need to purchase it?

Penal Substitution answers that we were *purchased from God's wrath*. A proof text of this would be Romans 5:9 "Much more then, having now been justified by His blood, we shall be saved from wrath through Him." But this will not work either. This verse is not saying that at the cross, in the past, Jesus death appeased God's wrath. It is saying that in the future, when the wrath of God comes upon the ungodly, we will be saved because we have been made just/righteous, friends of Jesus, and will not be among those who come under wrath. Deliverance and ransom are very closely related thoughts. In Galatians 1:4, "[Jesus] gave Himself for our sins" —not to deliver us from the hands of an angry father—but "that He might deliver us from this present evil age."

The most important part of the metaphor to keep in mind is that the Lord *bought* us. That means He owns us. We are not our own, but have been bought with a price.[1] So we belong to Him and we get to serve as His servants. What a privilege!

Remission/Forgiveness

The Greek noun *aphesis* is translated nine times as "remission" and six times as "forgiveness" in the KJV.[2] In Luke 4:18, *aphesis* is "deliverance" (to the captives) and "liberty" (to those

---

[1] 1 Corinthians 6:20
[2] Wycliffe's A.D. 1388 translation uses "remission" sixteen times and "forgiveness" once.

who are bruised).

Its primary meaning is releasing or setting free.[1] In the Septuagint, *aphesis* was used to translate the Year of Jubilee. In the Year of Jubilee, slaves were set free, debts were cancelled, and property went back to the former owners. So, in Greek, this became the "Year of Remission."

Older translations tend to translate *aphesis* more commonly as "remission", and newer translations tend to use "forgiveness". These words overlap in meaning, but their emphases are different.

The English word "forgive" has a primary meaning of "to cease to feel resentment against an offender."[2] This is a bit different than releasing someone. I can forgive my child for doing wrong, but still punish him because he needs to be taught a lesson. However, remission or release would set the child free of punishment. Although "forgiveness" appeals more to our Western preoccupation with guilt, "forgiveness" is generally not a fully adequate translation for *aphesis*. "Remission" or "release" is a better translation.

Of course, remission of sins includes forgiveness from God, but the emphasis is on the taking away of sins. Jesus' blood removes our sins, washing them away, thus setting us free. So when Jesus says in Matthew 26:28,

> For this is My blood of the new covenant, which is shed for many for the remission (*aphesis*) of sins,

He is referring to the fact that his blood sets us free (by washing

---

[1] Friberg's lexicon gives it a primary meaning (1) of captivity *release, liberation, deliverance. Analytical Lexicon of the Greek New Testament,* s.v. "Remission," Grand Rapids, MI: Baker Books, 2000
[2] Webster's New Collegiate Dictionary, 1977, s.v. "forgive"

us).

When Colossians 1:14 says,

> in whom we have redemption through His blood, the forgiveness (*aphesis*) of sins.

I believe the translators have missed the mark. Jesus' blood *redeems* us (from the power of darkness of the previous verse) by *releasing* us from our sins. (We are forgiven based on our repentance.) The way that Jesus' blood releases us from sins is by *cleansing* us of them. Hebrews 9:14 says, "How much more shall the blood of Christ . . . *cleanse* your conscience from dead works to serve the living God?" (emphasis added).

Sacrifice

Penal Substitution sees the sacrifice of Jesus as a *ritualistic* sacrifice. However, the New Testament images are better explained by seeing his death as a *heroic* sacrifice.[1] A ritualistic sacrifice is one where the anger of a deity is appeased or his favor is gained by the slaying of a victim. A heroic sacrifice is one in which someone lays down his rights, preferences, or life on behalf of others. In Romans 12:1, we are told to present our bodies as a "living sacrifice." In Philippians 2:15, the Philippians' shining as lights to the world is described as the sacrifice and service of their faith. The Scriptures are comfortable seeing sacrifice in terms of heroic selflessness in addition to cultic offering.

Scapegoat

---

[1] Bercot, *What the Early Christians Believed about the Atonement*

A scapegoat[1] in Tyndale's coinage, literally means "escape goat"—the goat that escapes. This is because it was sent out to the wilderness to never return. However, the term has morphed to mean "one who bears the blame for others." I have no problem with this meaning—it is just an interesting example of how word meanings change. Because people focus more on the fact that the goat was symbolically carrying people's sins into the wilderness than about the fact that it was "escaping", the word "scapegoat" came to mean bearing others' blame.

It is common to hear people say that in this Day of Atonement ritual, two goats were used to make a picture that is fulfilled in Christ's death. It is said that both goats represent Christ, but that it took one to be sacrificed and one to be sent away bearing sins to complete this picture. This is a possible interpretation, but unfortunately, the New Testament does not explain the ritual. Jesus is often called "the Lamb of God." He is nowhere called our scapegoat. Several different suggestions have been made, but it seems unlikely that the scapegoat ritual was important to understanding Christ's work, or we would expect that the New Testament would refer to it.

Sin/Sin offering

2 Corinthians 5:21 says, "[God] made Him [Christ] who knew no sin to be sin for us, that we might become the righteousness of God in Him."

The Penal Substitution model proposes that God somehow put sin on Jesus on the cross, and that was why his wrath could

---

[1] There is debate about the meaning of the Hebrew word for scapegoat (*la-azazel*). The Septuagint translators felt it meant "the sent away one." Some have argued it is the "goat for Azazel," and suggest that Azazel is a demon god in the wilderness.

come down on his Son. Notice, however, that it doesn't say that Jesus *became sinful* for us. What "became sin" could mean is quite obscure (in English). However, this mystery can be solved by the insight that the Greek word here, *hamartia*, is used in the Septuagint in a specific way.

Ninety-four times in the Septuagint, *hamartia* is used to translate the Hebrew word for "sin-offering."[1] Paul used and quoted from the Septuagint. There is no reason not to assume that he is using the word *hamartia* in 2 Corinthians 5:21 in the way with which he was familiar. "He made Him who knew no sin to be a sin-offering for us"—in other words, an offering on behalf of sins.

The sin-offering in Leviticus 4 is said to make atonement for sins. Since the Hebrew root for the word translated as "make atonement" (*kaphar*) means "to cover" or "to wash away", we know that the sin offering was seen as covering or cleansing sins. However, we learn from Hebrews 10:1-4 that the blood of bulls and goats actually had no such power. The sin-offering was given as a picture. God forgave people based on their repentance, which they demonstrated by obediently sacrificing as he commanded them to do. He was pleased with the heart attitude of the people. He took no pleasure in the sacrifices themselves.[2],[3]

However, when Christ comes as the perfect sin-offering, he is able to take away sins. "For by one offering [for sin, i.e. sin-offering] He has perfected forever those who are being sanctified."[4] Jesus became an offering to take away sins—a sin offering.

---

[1] Stauffer, p. 29
[2] Hebrews 10:8
[3] Psalm 51:16, 17
[4] Hebrews 10:14, and see v. 12

The Blood of Jesus

Blood signifies life. The life of the flesh is in the blood. When an animal was sacrificed, it was giving its life, which was symbolized by the giving of its blood. Jesus said, "unless you eat the flesh of the Son of Man and drink His blood, you have no life in you."[1] Of course, this is to be taken spiritually, not physically. What he is saying is that if you don't have his resurrection life (Spirit) in you, you have no life. (He said, "I am the . . . Life.") "Much more then, being justified by His blood, we shall be saved from wrath through him."[2] I understand this statement to mean that we are justified (made just) by Jesus' blood to mean that his resurrection life given to us and working in us makes us just/righteous.

The blood of Jesus is powerful. In the Scriptures, the blood of Jesus is said to give life, to cleanse from sin, to save us, and to justify us.[3]

Blood symbolizes giving of life. We need Jesus' life in us to cleanse us. Blood cleanses. The Jewish sacrificial system was not picturing wrath against the animal, but rather the animal giving its life, contained in its blood, to those who have lost their spiritual life through sin. Laying hands on the sacrifice implies identification with it. The slaying had little significance—it was simply necessary for obtaining the blood

---

[1] John 6:53
[2] Romans 5:9
[3] Why are Satan worshipers attracted to blood in their rituals? Here's a response from a man who claimed to be a sorcerer: "Why do you need to use blood? Because blood is life. It has an energy, a life force. So Demons are attracted to it. Plus, it gives them some substance to take some form. If only you could see the demons attracted to the fresh corpses of the newly killed on the battlefield in times of war." I do not recommend going to sorcerers for information, but it is interesting that according to this, they are not using blood simply for the sake of cruelty but because they claim that there is power in blood.

and the flesh, which were the focus of the rites and implied the giving of life. In Leviticus 17:11, it is the blood that makes atonement—by reason of its life—given to us, and giving us life.

Life, Spirit, and blood are connected in their significance for man's salvation and restoration. Blood and Spirit (and water) agree in one.[1]

Blood protects us. The blood of the Passover lamb was a protection, rather than an appeasement to deflect God's wrath. We should not equate the need for the blood of Jesus with an idea that God needed to punish him for sins.

---

[1] 1 John 5:6

Appendix B

Penal Substitution Proof Texts Examined

We have touched on a number of passages that are often taken to support Penal Substitution, and there are others we have not. There is not time to go through every Scripture in detail that has been or could be fitted into a Penal Substitution framework. However, we will look at some of the prominent verses, and if you come across a verse that is not addressed here, perhaps these will give ideas for how to interpret others.

Isaiah 53 is really the go-to passage for Penal Substitution. There are several phrases that are interpreted as God's wrath coming down on Jesus. Most notable are the following verses of this chapter:

> 6 . . .And the Lord has laid on Him the iniquity of us all.
>
> 10 Yet it pleased the Lord to bruise Him;
> He has put Him to grief. . .
>
> 11 He shall see the labor of His soul, and be satisfied. . .

It is important to note what these verses do *not* say. Although they can sound like they support Penal Substitution, they do not say that Jesus suffered the wrath of God. They do not say that he made a payment for sin, and they do not say he was punished for our sins.

Here is how I understand Isaiah 53:5-11:

verse 5: Jesus was crucified, wounded, and bruised on behalf of our sins. We are given spiritual healing through his atoning work.

verse 6: The marginal reference says, "Literally, the Lord has caused to land on him the iniquity of us all."[1] This could be the sins that were sinned against him. More likely however, it refers to the fact that Jesus died as the consequence of our sin. Had we not sinned; no atonement would have been needed. Jesus died as a result of our sin. Thus, our iniquity landed on him.

verse 8: He was stricken *because of* or *on behalf of* our transgressions. There is no need to see God as pouring wrath out on Jesus here.

verse 10a: "It pleased the Lord to bruise Him. . ."—God is ultimately sovereign over all. He can prevent what he will, and allow what he will. It was his will for Jesus to suffer and die because that was the only way for us to be saved. In the sense that Jesus went to suffer and die at the hands of wicked men at the bidding of his Father, it was the Father who put him to pain and who laid on him the burden of our iniquity to endure and carry away. Of course God was pleased to see his Son pass the test! It pleased the Lord to allow his Son to be bruised. Not that his Son's pain was pleasing to him, but the Father was cheering his Son on and pleased that he did so well.

Did Satan bring trouble upon Job, or did God? As we read the

---

[1] NKJV, Thomas Nelson

account, it certainly sounds as if Satan was responsible. Yet in allowing Satan to do this, God takes responsibility upon himself. And so, in Job 2:3 God says, "And still he holds fast to his integrity, although you [Satan] incited Me [God] against him, to destroy him without cause." The phrase, "It pleased the Lord to bruise him" must be seen in light of the New Testament verses that lay the guilt of killing Jesus on the Jewish leaders.

verse 11: "He shall see the labor of His soul, and be satisfied." This is a case where it appears that the Masoretic text has been corrupted. The Dead Sea Isaiah Scroll, a thousand years earlier than our earliest Masoretic texts, has this verse as:

> Out of the suffering of his soul he will see light, and find satisfaction. And through his knowledge his servant, the righteous one, will make many righteous, and he will bear their iniquities.[1]

This verse is not saying that God's wrath was satisfied because of Jesus' sufferings. In its earliest Hebrew form as recorded in the Dead Sea Scroll, it is Jesus himself who will be satisfied! Did you notice the verse at the very beginning of this book?

> Jesus who died shall be satisfied,
> And earth and Heav'n be one![2]

So, while it is possible to import the idea of God's wrath into these verses, and that wrath coming down on Jesus, it is not necessary. They can be read as God in Christ, heroically laying down his life on behalf of the many, and pleasing his Father by doing so.

It is also worth pointing out that for hundreds of millions of

---

[1] Isaiah 53:11 ISV; Copyright © 1995-2014 by ISV Foundation. ALL RIGHTS RESERVED INTERNATIONALLY. Used by permission of Davidson Press, LLC.
[2] Maltie D. Babcock

Orthodox Christians who use a translation of the Septuagint Old Testament, Isaiah 53 reads quite differently. You can't get Penal Substitution out of the Septuagint version of this passage. Some credibility is given to the Septuagint version of this passage by the fact that when the New Testament quotes from Isaiah 53, it quotes from the Septuagint in Acts 8:32-33 and possibly Romans 4:25 ("Who was delivered over for our offences") and Romans 8:32 ("delivered Him up for us all").

Mark 15:34 "My God, My God, why have You forsaken Me?"

Penal Substitution understands this to mean that because the ugliness of sin was put upon Jesus, the Father could not bear to look at him, and turned his back on Jesus. Some would say that this was part of the wrath of God that Jesus had to bear—to be rejected by his Father.

Jesus is quoting Psalm 22:1. In the pain and torment and loneliness of that hour, perhaps it felt as if the Father had forsaken him. But the irony here is that this Psalm, which starts with the cry, "My God, My God, why have You forsaken Me," then goes on to declare that the Father had not forsaken the Son at all!

> For He has *not* despised nor abhorred the affliction of the afflicted;
> *Nor has He hidden His face from Him*;
> But when He cried to Him, *He heard.*[1]

This is probably the same event that is described in Psalm 18:6-7.

> In my distress I called upon the Lord,
> And cried out to my God;

---

[1] Psalm 22:24, emphasis added

He heard my voice from His temple,
And my cry came before Him, even to His ears.

Then the earth shook and trembled;
The foundations of the hills also quaked and were shaken,
Because He was angry.

This earth shaking is described in Matthew 27:51, and the proof that Lord heard from his temple (having not forsaken his Son) was the rending of the veil from the top to the bottom.

Have you ever, in some bitter hour of despair, pain, or torment felt as if God had forsaken you? Have you groped about in the dark, wondering if God could possibly be there? Looking back, you know that he was with you, even in that darkest hour when you could not see or hear or feel him. And you also know that Jesus understood and knew what you were feeling. He also was tested in every point as we are. It was necessary that he be able to empathize with those who feel forsaken by God. But as surely as you were not forsaken by God, neither was he.

If Mark 15:34 is taken as literal proof that the Father had actually forsaken the Son, then we should also take Jesus' word "why" as a real question, and say that he *didn't know why the Father had forsaken him.*[1] The idea that Jesus didn't know what was happening while he hung on the cross would be odd indeed!

If Penal Substitution were true, Jesus would have been more correct to call out, "My God! My God! Why are you _killing_ me!" If God the Father had forsaken Jesus, then he would not have been around to be pouring out wrath on him.

---

[1] Credit to Keith Crider for this observation. Keith Crider, *Sacrifice or Penalty? Why it matters what we believe about Christ's death.* (Harrisonburg, VA: Christian Light Publications, 2018), 45.

Roman 3:25 "Whom God set forth as a propitiation by His blood . . ." See Appendix A: "Propitiation/Mercy Seat."

Romans 5:9-10. "Much more then, having now been justified by His blood, we shall be saved from wrath through Him. For if, when we were enemies we were reconciled to God through the death of His Son, much more, having been reconciled, we shall be saved by His life."

Of course, if we have been made just/righteous, we will not come under God's wrath! This is future, eschatological salvation from future wrath. How were we reconciled by the death of his Son?

This verse highlighted for me just how deeply Penal Substitution influences our thought patterns. I had thought about it for years, until one day it suddenly became clear to me. I was trying to understand it objectively: what did Christ's death objectively change that brought reconciliation? Suddenly, I saw it should be understood subjectively. It was not God who was reconciled, it was we! We were God's enemies. God was not our enemy. How were we reconciled to God by the death of his Son? God offered his Son to die for us. When we saw that, we realized how deeply God loved us, and our hearts melted. Our hearts had to soften toward God before he could save us. However, it was the message of the cross that softened them.

It is really his resurrection (life) that saves us. But, the message that "Christ rose to save you" does not soften hearts much, because it doesn't sound that heroic or sacrificial. However, the message "Christ died to save you" softens our hearts and reconciles us to God. The change is subjective—in us. As soon as that surrender and reconciliation happens, the way is clear for his life to flow to us, and so—"Much more, having been reconciled, we shall be *saved by his life*" (emphasis added). Since there is now peace between us (we are no longer God's enemies because we saw how far he was willing to go and our hearts melted), how much more shall we be saved from sin and sinning by having his resurrection life coursing in our veins!

God showed us how far he was willing to go, how great was his mercy and goodwill, by allowing Jesus to be murdered without even intervening. That means that his goodwill toward us is great. Thus, we can be confident that if we come to him, since he has shown how merciful he is, he will receive us.

Romans 8:3 "For what the law could not do in that it was weak through the flesh, God did by sending His own Son in the likeness of sinful flesh, on account of sin: He condemned sin in the flesh."

Penal Substitution understands this to mean that God put sin on Jesus, then punished sin in Jesus' body, and thereby he condemned sin. However, if "condemned sin in the flesh" is taken to mean "punished sin in Jesus' flesh", the passage becomes contradictory.

What God did in Jesus was "what the law could not do". The law could (and did) condemn and punish sin. What the law could not do was give people the power to overcome sin. It could only tell them not to sin and punish them when they failed.

Jesus came in a body that was just like ours, having flesh. (However, it was not sinful flesh as ours is, so though it was actual flesh, it was only in the *likeness* of sinful flesh.) In his own nature, God cannot be tempted with sin. But when he took on our nature, it was possible for him to be tempted, and he was.

However, because he never sinned, he showed that flesh can be without sin. Furthermore, because he gives us his flesh, which overcame sin, he thereby gives us power over sin. So, because Jesus did not sin, he condemned (judged) sin in the flesh. There is no longer any excuse for it. If we walk according to the Spirit and power he supplies, the righteous requirement of the law can be fulfilled in us.[1]

2 Corinthians 5:21 "For He made Him who knew no sin to be sin for us."

Earlier, we looked at this verse under the heading, "Sin/Sin offering" and concluded that *hamartia* in this verse means that Jesus was made an offering on behalf of sin. If we took this verse as Penal Substitution does, we would have to say that Jesus was *made to be sin(ful)*. This is impossible. God cannot be sin. Penal Substitution teaches that our sins were imputed (reckoned) to Jesus, but that would not *make* him sin. It would mean he was *imputed* sin. I see no logical way to take this verse except to be saying that Jesus was made to be a sin-offering, on behalf of sin.

Galatians 3:13 "Christ has redeemed us from the curse of the law, having become a curse for us (for it is written, 'Cursed is everyone who hangs on a tree')".

Though this is a difficult passage, I cannot accept what R.C.

---

[1] The Greek *katakrino* (condemn) could also be taken in the sense of "overthrow." If that is the meaning, it would be saying that Jesus, coming in flesh like ours, but without sinning, thereby "overthrew" sin in the flesh.

Sproul said:

> God is too holy to even look at iniquity. God the Father turned His back on the Son, cursing Him to the pit of hell while on He hung on the cross. Here was the Son's "descent into hell." Here the fury of God raged against Him. His scream was the scream of the damned. For us.[1]

If the Father was weeping at his Son's pain, cheering him on, suffering with him as Jesus brought us salvation, and showing depths of mercy and suffering love by allowing evil men to do this, the above paragraph does a grave disservice to God's reputation.

The first odd thing about Galatians 3:13 is that Paul does not quote very accurately. Deuteronomy 21:23 says, "He who is hanged is accursed of God." Was Paul quoting in rather free form to deliberately avoid saying that Christ was accursed by God?

The "curse of the law" is referring to Deuteronomy 27:26, which is cited in Galatians 3:10.

> For as many as are of the works of the law are under the curse; for it is written, "Cursed is everyone who does not continue in all things which are written in the book of the law, to do them."

Paul says that all who are under the law are under a curse. Note carefully that he does not say, "*are* cursed" but "are *under* the curse." In other words, the curse is hanging over your head, and as soon as you disobey the law, *BAM!* The

---

[1] R.C. Sproul, "Treasuring Redemption's Price", Ligonier Ministries, accessed April 20, 2020. https://www.ligonier.org/learn/devotionals/treasuring-redemptions-price/

curse falls on you. This is a precarious position.[1] Christ allowed himself to suffer a humiliating, cursed death. Thereby he fulfilled the Old Covenant and removed its law, nailing it to his cross.[2] Because of that, we do not live under the Mosaic Law, but under the New Covenant. We are no longer under the curse of the Law, which is superseded. His pain brought our blessing. This is what the Atonement is all about.

Colossians 2:14 "Having wiped out the handwriting of requirements that was against us, which was contrary to us."

"Aha!" some would say. "Our problem was with the law after all" (rather than our need to be cleansed). True, we were transgressors and therefore in trouble with the law. This is one of the things that needed resolved. Jesus accomplished multiple things by his death. One of them was that he brought in a new and better covenant, and in so doing made the old obsolete. Wiping out the "handwriting of requirements" (the penalties of the old law that we had coming to us because of our sins) is just one of the consequences of bringing in a new covenant of life. Other things mentioned in the passage that Jesus' death accomplished are making us alive, forgiving (not paying for) our trespasses, and disarming principalities and powers.

Hebrews 9:14 "How much more shall the blood of Christ, who through the eternal Spirit offered Himself without spot to God, cleanse your conscience from dead works to

---

[1] This must be harmonized with Luke 1:5-6. Zacharias and Elizabeth were blameless with regard to the law. They had not been cursed by it, but they were under its system, and disobedience would bring the curse which they lived under, down upon them.
[2] Colossians 2:14

serve the living God?"

Here, some would see "offered Himself without spot to God" as confirmation that Jesus was giving himself as a ransom price to God, or to pay our penalty. However, this offering should be understood as specifically referring to Jesus' last words, "Father, into Your hands I commit My spirit."[1] He had completed his task, and had been made perfect by the things that he had suffered.[2] Having suffered all things without sin, he had thereby overcome all sin—and was still spotless! So he was able to offer his Spirit up to God, with no stain of sin on it, and that same Spirit could then be put into us to purge out the sin from our spirits. In Hebrews 9, the excitement is about the fact that because Jesus was spotless, he was able to enter the most holy place (probably heaven) and purge it (probably by casting Satan out). And because he ever lives there to make intercession for us, he is able to save us to the uttermost![3]

Hebrews 9:22 "Without shedding of blood there is no remission."

While this is often interpreted to mean that someone had to pay the penalty in blood, that is simply reading more into the verse than is there. There is no payment being suggested. Blood is needed, not for payment, but for remission, which means release from sins. However, this phrase is really lifted out of context. The full verse is, "And according to the law almost all things are purified with blood, and without shedding of blood there is no remission."

Here we have a problem. Leviticus 5:11-13 describes a sin-offering made of grain (without blood) and states that the

---

[1] Luke 23:46
[2] Hebrews 2:10, 5:8
[3] Hebrews 7:25

offerer will be forgiven. How can we harmonize this with Hebrews 9:22? Remember (as we discussed in Appendix A) that forgiveness and remission are not identical? It is possible, if not likely, that Hebrews 9:22 is actually referring to the Year of Jubilee, which was called the Year of Remission in the Septuagint.[1] There was no Year of Remission without shedding the blood of sacrificial offerings.

Even if the Year of Remission is not what the verse is referring to, we must remember that this is a specific statement about the Mosaic Law. I do not think that this is so much giving us a cosmic principle that "forgiveness requires blood" as it is pointedly saying that the law generally required blood-sacrifices to make atonement for sin. And this was ultimately to picture the fact that Jesus was going to give his own blood to remit (wash away) our sins. When Jesus forgave people of their sins in the Gospels, it seems unreasonable to think that he was only able to forgive them (right then and there) because he was anticipating shedding his blood at a future point. His blood did need to be shed at a future point to deal with the worldwide past, present, and future problem of sin. But if I can forgive someone right now for wronging me without shedding any blood, then surely Jesus could do the same.

1 Peter 2:24 "Who Himself bore our sins in His own body on the tree, that we, having died to sins, might live for righteousness."

Penal Substitution understands this to mean that our guilt was divinely put on Jesus so that divine punishment could come upon him. However, guilt is something experienced in the soul, not in the body. As we sinned against Jesus, however, he endured our sins against his physical body. On the cross, Jesus

---

[1] Credit to Mike Atnip for this observation, via personal email, 11/27/2017.

endured (bore) the actual sins that were committed against him. With mocking, scourging, thorns, and spitting, thousands of individual sins against his physical person were committed in the last 24 hours of his life. Just as he can be seen as our representative, dying for us, so his murderers can be seen as our representatives, doing to him what we would have done ourselves but for the grace of God. So in that very real sense, he bore our sins in, upon, and against his own body on the tree.

This verse could also be saying that Jesus carried our sins away to dispose of them.

> As far as the east is from the west,
> So far has He removed our transgressions from us.[1]

John the Baptist said, "Behold! The Lamb of God who takes away the sin of the world!"[2] In Numbers 18:1, Aaron and his sons are said to bear the iniquity of the sanctuary and of their priesthood. In Exodus 28:38, Aaron is commanded to bear the iniquity of the holy things. *Barnes' Notes on the Bible* comments on this verse that the Hebrew expression "to bear iniquity" is applied either to one who suffers the penalty of sin or to one who takes away the sin of others. In Leviticus 10:17 (KVV), the priests are said to bear the iniquity of the people. Whatever the priests bearing iniquity meant, it did not involve punishment for them. The scapegoat ritual could be understood as Jesus, carrying our sins away to dispose of them, like taking garbage away to the dump.

1 John 1:9 "If we confess our sins, He is faithful and just [*dikaios*] to forgive us our sins and to cleanse us from

---

[1] Psalm 103:12
[2] John 1:29

all unrighteousness."

It is said "Wouldn't we think that it would be mercy for him to forgive us our sins? But here we find that he is *just* to do so. Clearly, this is because Jesus paid for our sins, and to not get what he paid for would be an injustice. So, God is just to forgive us our sins." Remember, we are thinking of "just" in too narrow of a sense of getting what is deserved. The just/righteous thing to do is the "right" thing. God teaches us that it is right to show mercy to anyone who is repentant. So, it is *just* of him to show mercy in forgiving our sins!

1 John 2:2 "And He Himself *is* [not *was*] the propitiation for our sins, and not for ours only but also for the whole world."

"Propitiation" should be translated as "expiation" here. Jesus is the expiation for our sins—the means by which our sins are dealt with and removed. This is not referring to a past event, but rather, a present reality. As you come to God, Jesus washes away your sins in the present. It is not his *past sacrifice* that is the expiation John is referring to—although it took that past act to bring in everlasting righteousness. But the focus here is on the fact that he himself, right now takes away our sins. See Appendix A: "Propitiation/Mercy Seat."

Here are a few verses among many that we have looked at that make less sense under Penal Substitution.

Revelation 5:9 "And they sang a new song, saying, 'Worthy are

You to take the book and to break its seals; for You were slain, and purchased for God with Your blood men from every tribe and tongue and people and nation.'" (NASB)

"Purchased for God"—from God's wrath to God? This would be better understood as "purchased us to God from destruction", or possibly "from the devil".

Romans 8:32 "He who did not spare His own Son, but delivered Him up for us all, how shall He not with Him also freely give us all things?"

Did God deliver his Son up to himself?

John 12:31 "Now is the judgment of this world; now the ruler of this world will be cast out."

How does this fit into Penal Substitution?

1 John 3:5 "And you know that He was manifested to take away our sins, and in Him there is no sin."

He takes away our sins rather than is punished for them.

1 John 3:8 "For this purpose the Son of God was manifested, that He might destroy the works of the devil."

Romans 8:2 "For the law of the Spirit of life in Christ Jesus has made me free from the law of sin and death."

We are not free because of the satisfaction of the "law of punishment of sin," but because of the "law of the Spirit of life".

Appendix C

List of New Testament Atonement Verses

The following verses make specific statements about the Atonement. They speak about what Jesus did for us, and how and why. I culled these verses in a reading through the New Testament specifically for that purpose. It is likely that I missed some.

Verses showing that our need is *life*, not just for God to forgive us.

John 3:1-8 To be born is to enter into life. This whole passage about being born again shows that our need was for new life.

John 3:15 "that whoever believes in Him should not perish but have eternal life."

John 3:16 "For God so loved the world that He gave His only begotten Son, that whoever believes in Him should not perish but have everlasting life."

John 5:21 "For as the Father raises the dead and gives life to them, even so the Son gives life to whom He will."

John 5:24 "Most assuredly, I say to you, he who hears My word and believes in Him who sent Me has everlasting life, and shall not come into judgment, but has passed from death into life."

John 5:25 "Most assuredly, I say to you, the hour is coming, and now is, when the dead will hear the voice of the Son of God; and those who hear will live."

John 5:26 "For as the Father has life in Himself, so He has granted the Son to have life in Himself,"

John 5:40 "But you are not willing to come to Me that you may have life.

John 6:27 "Do not labor for the food which perishes, but for the food which endures to everlasting life, which the Son of Man will give you, because God the Father has set His seal on Him."

John 6:33 "For the bread of God is He who comes down from heaven and gives life to the world."

John 6:35 "And Jesus said to them, 'I am the bread of life. He who comes to Me shall never hunger, and he who believes in Me shall never thirst.'"

John 6:40 "And this is the will of Him who sent Me, that everyone who sees the Son and believes in Him may have everlasting life; and I will raise him up at the last day."

John 6:48-50 "I am the bread of life. Your fathers ate the manna in the wilderness, and are dead. This is the bread which comes down from heaven, that one may eat of it and not die."

John 6:51 "I am the living bread which came down from heaven. If anyone eats of this bread, he will live forever; and the bread that I shall give is My flesh, which I shall give for the life of the world."

John 6:53 "Then Jesus said to them, 'Most assuredly, I say to you, unless you eat the flesh of the Son of Man and drink His blood, you have no life in you.'"

John 6:54 "Whoever eats My flesh and drinks My blood has eternal life, and I will raise him up at the last day."

John 6:57 "As the living Father sent Me, and I live because of the Father, so he who feeds on Me will live because of Me."

John 6:63 "It is the Spirit who gives life; the flesh profits nothing. The words that I speak to you are spirit, and they are life."

John 7:38-39 "He who believes in Me, as the Scripture has said, out of his heart will flow rivers of living water. But this He spoke concerning the Spirit, whom those believing in Him would receive; for the Holy Spirit was not yet given, because Jesus was not yet glorified."

John 8:12 "Then Jesus spoke to them again, saying, 'I am the light of the world. He who follows Me shall not walk in darkness, but have the light of life.'"

John 8:51 "Most assuredly, I say to you, if anyone keeps My word he shall never see death."

John 10:10 "The thief does not come except to steal, and to kill, and to destroy. I have come that they may have life, and that they may have it more abundantly."

John 10:28 "And I give them eternal life, and they shall never perish; neither shall anyone snatch them out of My hand."

John 11:25 "Jesus said to her, 'I am the resurrection and the life. He who believes in Me, though he may die, he shall live.'"

John 11:26 "And whoever lives and believes in Me shall never die. Do you believe this?"

John 12:46 "I have come as a light into the world, that whoever believes in Me should not abide in darkness."

John 12:47 "And if anyone hears My words and does not believe, I do not judge him; for I did not come to judge the world but to save the world."

John 14:19 "A little while longer and the world will see Me no more, but you will see Me. Because I live, you will live also."

John 15: The image of the vine and branches is an image of life being given through the vine.

John 17:2 "as You have given Him authority over all flesh, that He should give eternal life to as many as You have given Him."

John 17:3 "And this is eternal life, that they may know You, the only true God, and Jesus Christ whom You have sent."

Acts 11:18 "When they heard these things they became silent; and they glorified God, saying, 'Then God has also granted to the Gentiles repentance to life.'"

Acts 13:46 "Then Paul and Barnabas grew bold and said, 'It was necessary that the word of God should be spoken to you first; but since you reject it, and judge yourselves unworthy of everlasting life, behold, we turn to the Gentiles.'"

Romans 5:10 "For if when we were enemies we were reconciled to God through the death of His Son, much more, having been reconciled, we shall be saved by His life."

Romans 8:2 "For the law of the Spirit of life in Christ Jesus has made me free from the law of sin and death."

Romans 8:9-10 "But you are not in the flesh but in the Spirit, if indeed the Spirit of God dwells in you. Now if anyone does not have the Spirit of Christ, he is not His. And if Christ is in you, the body is dead because of sin, but the Spirit is life because of righteousness."

Romans 8:11 "But if the Spirit of Him who raised Jesus from the dead dwells in you, He who raised Christ from the dead will also give life to your mortal bodies through His Spirit who dwells in you."

Romans 5:17 "For if by the one man's offense death reigned through the one, much more those who receive abundance of grace and of the gift of righteousness will reign in life through the One, Jesus Christ."

Romans 7:11 "For sin, taking occasion by the commandment, deceived me, and by it killed me." *(So I needed to be given life).*

Because Jesus said that we must eat his flesh and drink his blood to have life, the next four verses are related to the theme of our need for life.

1 Corinthians 10:2-4 "all were baptized into Moses in the cloud and in the sea, all ate the same spiritual food, and all drank the same spiritual drink. For they drank of that spiritual Rock that followed them, and that Rock was Christ."

1 Corinthians 11:25 "In the same manner He also took the cup after supper, saying, 'This cup is the new covenant in My blood. This do, as often as you drink it, in remembrance of Me.'"

1 Corinthians 12:13 "For by one Spirit we were all baptized into one body—whether Jews or Greeks, whether slaves or free—and have all been made to drink into one Spirit."

1 Corinthians 15:45 "And so it is written, 'The first man Adam became a living being.' The last Adam became a life-giving spirit."

Colossians 3:4 "When Christ who is our life appears, then you also will appear with Him in glory."

1 Timothy 6:12 "Fight the good fight of faith, lay hold on eternal life, to which you were also called and have confessed the good confession in the presence of many witnesses."

1 Timothy 6:13 "I urge you in the sight of God who gives life to all things, and before Christ Jesus who witnessed the good confession before Pontius Pilate,"

2 Timothy 1:10 "but has now been revealed by the appearing of our Savior Jesus Christ, who has abolished death and brought life and immortality to light through the gospel,"

Colossians 3:3 "For you died, and your life is hidden with Christ in God."

Colossians 3:4 "When Christ who is our life appears, then you also will appear with Him in glory."

1 Thessalonians 5:10 "who died for us, that whether we wake or sleep, we should live together with Him."

2 Timothy 2:11 "This is a faithful saying: For if we died with Him, We shall also live with Him."

Titus 1:2 "in hope of eternal life which God, who cannot lie, promised before time began,"

Hebrews 7:16 "who has come, not according to the law of a fleshly commandment, but according to the power of an endless life."

Hebrews 7:25 "Therefore He is also able to save to the uttermost those who come to God through Him, since He always lives to make intercession for them."

1 John 1:2 "the life was manifested, and we have seen, and bear witness, and declare to you that eternal life which was with the Father and was manifested to us"

1 John 3:8 "He who sins is of the devil, for the devil has sinned from the beginning. For this purpose the Son of God was manifested, that He might destroy the works of the devil."

1 John 5:11 "And this is the testimony: that God has given us eternal life, and this life is in His Son."

1 John 5:12 "He who has the Son has life; he who does not have the Son of God does not have life."

1 John 5:13 "These things I have written to you who believe in the name of the Son of God, that you may know that you have eternal life, and that you may continue to believe in the name of the Son of God."

1 John 5:16 "If anyone sees his brother sinning a sin which does not lead to death, he will ask, and He will give him life for those who commit sin not leading to death. There is sin leading to death. I do not say that he should pray about that."

1 John 5:20 "And we know that the Son of God has come and has given us an understanding, that we may know Him who is true; and we are in Him who is true, in His Son Jesus Christ. This is the true God and eternal life."

Verses showing the meaning of his life and ministry (may extend to his death also)

Matthew 18:11 "For the Son of Man has come to save that which was lost."

Mark 1:38 "But He said to them, "Let us go into the next towns, that I may preach there also, because for this purpose I have come forth."

Luke 4:18 "The Spirit of the LORD is upon Me,
Because He has anointed Me
To preach the gospel to the poor;
He has sent Me to heal the brokenhearted,
To proclaim liberty to the captives
And recovery of sight to the blind,
To set at liberty those who are oppressed;"

Luke 4:19 "To proclaim the acceptable year of the LORD."

Luke 5:32 "I have not come to call the righteous, but sinners, to repentance."

Luke 9:56 "For the Son of Man did not come to destroy men's lives but to save them." And they went to another village.

Luke 12:49 "I came to send fire on the earth, and how I wish it were already kindled!"

Luke 12:51 "Do you suppose that I came to give peace on earth? I tell you, not at all, but rather division."

Luke 19:10 "for the Son of Man has come to seek and to save that which was lost."

Luke 19:12 "Therefore He said: 'A certain nobleman went into a far country to receive for himself a kingdom and to return.'"

Luke 22:27 "For who is greater, he who sits at the table, or he who serves? Is it not he who sits at the table? Yet I am among you as the One who serves."

John 3:17 "For God did not send His Son into the world to condemn the world, but that the world through Him might be saved."

John 9:39 "And Jesus said, 'For judgment I have come into this world, that those who do not see may see, and that those who see may be made blind.'"

John 10:10 "The thief does not come except to steal, and to kill, and to destroy. I have come that they may have life, and that they may have it more abundantly."

Acts 3:26 "To you first, God, having raised up His Servant Jesus, sent Him to bless you, in turning away every one of you from your iniquities."

Verses showing the meaning of Jesus' death

As a ransom

Matthew 20:28 "just as the Son of Man did not come to be served, but to serve, and to give His life a ransom for many."

Mark 10:45 "For even the Son of Man did not come to be served, but to serve, and to give His life a ransom for many."

1 Timothy 2:6 "who gave Himself a ransom for all, to be testified in due time,"

As a redemption:

Acts 20:28 "Therefore take heed to yourselves and to all the flock, among which the Holy Spirit has made you overseers, to shepherd the church of God which He purchased with His own blood."

Romans 3:24 "being justified freely by His grace through the redemption that is in Christ Jesus,"

1 Corinthians 1:30 "But of Him you are in Christ Jesus, who became for us wisdom from God– and righteousness and sanctification and redemption"

Galatians 4:5 "to redeem those who were under the law, that we might receive the adoption as sons."

Ephesians 1:7 "In Him we have redemption through His blood, the forgiveness of sins, according to the riches of His grace"

Ephesians 1:14 "who is the guarantee of our inheritance until the redemption of the purchased possession, to the praise of His glory."

Ephesians 4:30 "And do not grieve the Holy Spirit of God, by whom you were sealed for the day of redemption."

Colossians 1:14 "in whom we have redemption through His blood, the forgiveness of sins."

Titus 2:14 "who gave Himself for us, that He might redeem us from every lawless deed and purify for Himself His own special people, zealous for good works."

Hebrews 9:12 "Not with the blood of goats and calves, but with His own blood He entered the Most Holy Place once for all, having obtained eternal redemption."

Hebrews 9:15 "And for this reason He is the Mediator of the new covenant, by means of death, for the redemption of the transgressions under the first covenant, that those who are called may receive the promise of the eternal inheritance."

As a sacrifice, or for cleansing

Matthew 26:28 "For this is My blood of the new covenant, which is shed for many for the remission of sins."

Mark 14:24 "And He said to them, 'This is My blood of the new covenant, which is shed for many.'"

Luke 22:19 "And He took bread, gave thanks and broke it, and gave it to them, saying, 'This is My body which is given for you; do this in remembrance of Me.'"

Luke 22:20 "Likewise He also took the cup after supper, saying, 'This cup is the new covenant in My blood, which is shed for you.'"

John 1:29 "The next day John saw Jesus coming toward him, and said, 'Behold! The Lamb of God who takes away the sin of the world!'"

Romans 3:25 "whom God set forth as a propitiation by His blood, through faith, to demonstrate His righteousness, because in His forbearance God had passed over the sins that were previously committed,"

1 Corinthians 5:7 "Therefore purge out the old leaven, that you may be a new lump, since you truly are unleavened. For indeed Christ, our Passover, was sacrificed for us."

1 Corinthians 11:25 "In the same manner He also took the cup after supper, saying, 'This cup is the new covenant in My blood. This do, as often as you drink it, in remembrance of Me.'"

Ephesians 5:2 "And walk in love, as Christ also has loved us and given Himself for us, an offering and a sacrifice to God for a sweet-smelling aroma."

Hebrews 2:10 "For it was fitting for Him, for whom are all things and by whom are all things, in bringing many sons to glory, to make the captain of their salvation perfect through sufferings."

Hebrews 9:14 "how much more shall the blood of Christ, who through the eternal Spirit offered Himself without spot to God, cleanse your conscience from dead works to serve the living God?"

Hebrews 9:26 "He then would have had to suffer often since the foundation of the world; but now, once at the end of the ages, He has appeared to put away sin by the sacrifice of Himself."

Hebrews 9:28 "so Christ was offered once to bear the sins of many. To those who eagerly wait for Him He will appear a second time, apart from sin, for salvation."

Hebrews 10:10 "By that will we have been sanctified through the offering of the body of Jesus Christ once for all."

Hebrews 10:12 "But this Man, after He had offered one sacrifice for sins forever, sat down at the right hand of God,"

Hebrews 10:14 "For by one offering He has perfected forever those who are being sanctified."

1 John 1:7 "But if we walk in the light as He is in the light, we have fellowship with one another, and the blood of Jesus Christ His Son cleanses us from all sin."

1 John 2:2 "And He Himself is the propitiation for our sins, and not for ours only but also for the whole world."

1 John 4:10 "In this is love, not that we loved God, but that He loved us and sent His Son to be the propitiation for our sins."

1 John 1:9 "If we confess our sins, He is faithful and just to forgive us our sins and to cleanse us from all unrighteousness."

Priestly role

Romans 8:34 "Who is he who condemns? It is Christ who died, and furthermore is also risen, who is even at the right hand of God, who also makes intercession for us."

Ephesians 2:18 "For through Him we both have access by one Spirit to the Father."

Hebrews 1:3 "who being the brightness of His glory and the express image of His person, and upholding all things by the word of His power, when He had by Himself purged our sins, sat down at the right hand of the Majesty on high,"

Hebrews 2:9 "But we see Jesus, who was made a little lower than the angels, for the suffering of death crowned with glory and honor, that He, by the grace of God, might taste death for everyone."

Hebrews 2:10 "For it was fitting for Him, for whom are all things and by whom are all things, in bringing many sons to glory, to make the captain of their salvation perfect through sufferings."

Hebrews 2:17 "Therefore, in all things He had to be made like His brethren, that He might be a merciful and faithful High Priest in things pertaining to God, to make propitiation for the sins of the people."

Hebrews 2:18 "For in that He Himself has suffered, being tempted, He is able to aid those who are tempted."

Hebrews 5:8 "though He was a Son, yet He learned obedience by the things which He suffered."

Hebrews 5:9 "And having been perfected, He became the author of eternal salvation to all who obey Him,"

Hebrews 6:20 "where the forerunner has entered for us, even Jesus, having become High Priest forever according to the order of Melchizedek."

Hebrews 7:16 "who has come, not according to the law of a fleshly commandment, but according to the power of an endless life."

Hebrews 7:25 "Therefore He is also able to save to the uttermost those who come to God through Him, since He always lives to make intercession for them."

Hebrews 9:12 "Not with the blood of goats and calves, but with His own blood He entered the Most Holy Place once for all, having obtained eternal redemption."

Hebrews 10:14 "For by one offering He has perfected forever those who are being sanctified."

Hebrews 10:20 "by a new and living way which He consecrated for us, through the veil, that is, His flesh,"

To acquire kingship

Matthew 28:18 "And Jesus came and spoke to them, saying, "All authority has been given to Me in heaven and on earth."

John 5:27 "and has given Him authority to execute judgment also, because He is the Son of Man"

John 18:37 "Pilate therefore said to Him, 'Are You a king then?' Jesus answered, 'You say rightly that I am a king. For this cause I was born, and for this cause I have come into the world, that I should bear witness to the truth. Everyone who is of the truth hears My voice.'"

You have to believe on Jesus to be saved. In Acts, the focus is on his resurrection, because the resurrection proves that he is now the King. The thing you must believe is that Jesus is the King, because if you do, you will serve him (assumed).

Acts 2:30 "Therefore, being a prophet, and knowing that God had sworn with an oath to him that of the fruit of his body, according to the flesh, He would raise up the Christ to sit on his throne,"

Acts 5:31 "Him God has exalted to His right hand to be Prince and Savior, to give repentance to Israel and forgiveness of sins."

Romans 14:9 "For to this end Christ died and rose and lived again, that He might be Lord of both the dead and the living." (*This might be the best summary of all!*)

Luke 19:12 "Therefore He said: 'A certain nobleman went into a far country to receive for himself a kingdom and to return.'"

Ephesians 1:20-21 "which He worked in Christ when He raised Him from the dead and seated Him at His right hand in the heavenly places, far above all principality and power and might and dominion, and every name that is named, not only in this age but also in that which is to come."

Ephesians 1:22-23 "And He put all things under His feet, and gave Him to be head over all things to the church, which is His body, the fullness of Him who fills all in all."

Philippians 2:8-11 "And being found in appearance as a man, He humbled Himself and became obedient to the point of death, even the death of the cross. Therefore God also has highly exalted Him and given Him the name which is above every name, that at the name of Jesus every knee should bow, of those in heaven, and of those on earth, and of those under the earth, and that every tongue should confess that Jesus Christ is Lord, to the glory of God the Father."

Colossians 1:18 "And He is the head of the body, the church, who is the beginning, the firstborn from the dead, that in all things He may have the preeminence."

1 Peter 3:22 "who has gone into heaven and is at the right hand of God, angels and authorities and powers having been made subject to Him."

Revelation 5:9-10 "And they sang a new song, saying: "You are worthy to take the scroll, And to open its seals; For You were slain, And have redeemed us to God by Your blood Out of every tribe and tongue and people and nation, And have made us kings and priests to our God; And we shall reign on the earth."

Revelation 5:12 "saying with a loud voice: 'Worthy is the Lamb who was slain To receive power and riches and wisdom, And strength and honor and glory and blessing!'" *(His worthiness appears to be the result of being slain).*

To Become something

Hebrews 2:10 "For it was fitting for Him, for whom are all things and by whom are all things, in bringing many sons to glory, to make the captain of their salvation perfect through sufferings."

Hebrews 5:9 "And having been perfected, He became the author of eternal salvation to all who obey Him,"

Hebrews 7:28 "For the law appoints as high priests men who have weakness, but the word of the oath, which came after the law, appoints the Son who has been perfected forever."

To conquer Satan

John 12:31-32 "Now is the judgment of this world; now the ruler of this world will be cast out. And I, if I am lifted up from the earth, will draw all peoples to Myself."

Acts 26:18 "to open their eyes, in order to turn them from darkness to light, and from the power of Satan to God, that they may receive forgiveness of sins and an inheritance among those who are sanctified by faith in Me."

Colossians 2:15 "Having disarmed principalities and powers, He made a public spectacle of them, triumphing over them in it."

Hebrews 2:14 "Inasmuch then as the children have partaken of flesh and blood, He Himself likewise shared in the same, that through death He might destroy him who had the power of death, that is, the devil,"

Hebrews 2:15 "and release those who through fear of death were all their lifetime subject to bondage."

1 John 3:8 "He who sins is of the devil, for the devil has sinned from the beginning. For this purpose the Son of God was manifested, that He might destroy the works of the devil."

Identification with Christ

Romans 6: The Baptism passage is about salvation through identification with Christ.

Romans 7:4 "Therefore, my brethren, you also have become dead to the law through the body of Christ, that you may be married to another– to Him who was raised from the dead, that we should bear fruit to God."

Romans 13:14 "But put on the Lord Jesus Christ, and make no provision for the flesh, to fulfill its lusts."

1 Corinthians 15:22 "For as in Adam all die, even so in Christ all shall be made alive."

2 Corinthians 4:10 "always carrying about in the body the dying of the Lord Jesus, that the life of Jesus also may be manifested in our body."

2 Corinthians 4:11 "For we who live are always delivered to death for Jesus' sake, that the life of Jesus also may be manifested in our mortal flesh."

2 Corinthians 5:14-15 "For the love of Christ compels us, because we judge thus: that if One died for all, then all died; and He died for all, that those who live should live no longer for themselves, but for Him who died for them and rose again."

2 Corinthians 13:4 "For though He was crucified in weakness, yet He lives by the power of God. For we also are weak in Him, but we shall live with Him by the power of God toward you."

Galatians 6:14 "But God forbid that I should boast except in the cross of our Lord Jesus Christ, by whom the world has been crucified to me, and I to the world."

Ephesians 1:23 "which is His body, the fullness of Him who fills all in all."

Ephesians 2:5-6 "even when we were dead in trespasses, made us alive together with Christ (by grace you have been saved), and raised us up together, and made us sit together in the heavenly places in Christ Jesus,"

Ephesians 5:23 "For the husband is head of the wife, as also Christ is head of the church; and He is the Savior of the body."

Ephesians 5:30 "For we are members of His body, of His flesh and of His bones."

Philippians 3:10 "that I may know Him and the power of His resurrection, and the fellowship of His sufferings, being conformed to His death,"

Philippians 3:12 "Not that I have already attained, or am already perfected; but I press on, that I may lay hold of that for which Christ Jesus has also laid hold of me."

Colossians 1:22 "in the body of His flesh through death, to present you holy, and blameless, and above reproach in His sight"

Colossians 1:27 "To them God willed to make known what are the riches of the glory of this mystery among the Gentiles: which is Christ in you, the hope of glory."

Colossians 2:9 "For in Him dwells all the fullness of the Godhead bodily; 10 and you are complete in Him"

Colossians 2:12 "buried with Him in baptism, in which you also were raised with Him through faith in the working of God, who raised Him from the dead."

Colossians 2:13 "And you, being dead in your trespasses and the uncircumcision of your flesh, He has made alive together with Him, having forgiven you all trespasses,"

Colossians 2:20 "Therefore, if you died with Christ from the basic principles of the world, why, as though living in the world, do you subject yourselves to regulations"

Colossians 3:1 "If then you were raised with Christ, seek those things which are above, where Christ is, sitting at the right hand of God."

Colossians 3:3 "For you died, and your life is hidden with Christ in God."

Colossians 3:4 "When Christ who is our life appears, then you also will appear with Him in glory."

1 Thessalonians 5:10 "who died for us, that whether we wake or sleep, we should live together with Him."

2 Timothy 2:11 "This is a faithful saying: For if we died with Him, We shall also live with Him."

Hebrews 2:9 "But we see Jesus, who was made a little lower than the angels, for the suffering of death crowned with glory and honor, that He, by the grace of God, might taste death for everyone."

1 Peter 2:21-25 "For to this you were called, because Christ also suffered for us, leaving us an example, that you should follow His steps: Who committed no sin, Nor was deceit found in His mouth; who, when He was reviled, did not revile in return; when He suffered, He did not threaten, but committed Himself to Him who judges righteously; who Himself bore our sins in His own body on the tree, that we, having died to sins, might live for righteousness– by whose stripes you were healed. For you were like sheep going astray, but have now returned to the

Shepherd and Overseer of your souls."

1 Peter 3:18 "For Christ also suffered once for sins, the just for the unjust, that He might bring us to God, being put to death in the flesh but made alive by the Spirit,"

1 Peter 3:21 "There is also an antitype which now saves us–baptism (not the removal of the filth of the flesh, but the answer of a good conscience toward God), through the resurrection of Jesus Christ,"

2 Peter 1:4 "by which have been given to us exceedingly great and precious promises, that through these you may be partakers of the divine nature, having escaped the corruption that is in the world through lust."

For our sins

Matthew 26:28 "For this is My blood of the new covenant, which is shed for many for the remission of sins."

John 1:29 "The next day John saw Jesus coming toward him, and said, 'Behold! The Lamb of God who takes away the sin of the world!'"

Romans 3:25 "whom God set forth as a propitiation by His blood, through faith, to demonstrate His righteousness, because in His forbearance God had passed over the sins that were previously committed,"

1 Corinthians 15:3 "For I delivered to you first of all that which I also received: that Christ died for our sins according to the Scriptures,"

2 Corinthians 5:19 "that is, that God was in Christ reconciling the world to Himself, not imputing their trespasses to them, and has committed to us the word of reconciliation."

2 Corinthians 5:21 "For He made Him who knew no sin to be sin for us, that we might become the righteousness of God in Him."

Galatians 1:4 "who gave Himself for our sins, that He might deliver us from this present evil age, according to the will of our God and Father,"

Ephesians 1:7 "In Him we have redemption through His blood, the forgiveness of sins, according to the riches of His grace"

Hebrews 9:28 "so Christ was offered once to bear the sins of many. To those who eagerly wait for Him He will appear a second time, apart from sin, for salvation."

1 Peter 2:24 "who Himself bore our sins in His own body on the tree, that we, having died to sins, might live for righteousness– by whose stripes you were healed. For you were like sheep going astray, but have now returned to the Shepherd and Overseer of your souls."

1 Peter 3:18 "For Christ also suffered once for sins, the just for the unjust, that He might bring us to God, being put to death in the flesh but made alive by the Spirit,"

1 John 2:2 "And He Himself is the propitiation for our sins, and not for ours only but also for the whole world."

1 John 3:5 "And you know that He was manifested to take away our sins, and in Him there is no sin."

1 John 4:10 "In this is love, not that we loved God, but that He loved us and sent His Son to be the propitiation for our sins."

With reference to the law

Romans 7:4 "Therefore, my brethren, you also have become dead to the law through the body of Christ, that you may be married to another—to Him who was raised from the dead, that we should bear fruit to God."

Ephesians 2:15 "having abolished in His flesh the enmity, that is, the law of commandments contained in ordinances, so as to create in Himself one new man from the two, thus making peace,"

Ephesians 2:16 "and that He might reconcile them both to God in one body through the cross, thereby putting to death the enmity."

Ephesians 2:18 "For through Him we both have access by one Spirit to the Father."

Galatians 3:13 "Christ has redeemed us from the curse of the law, having become a curse for us (for it is written, 'Cursed is everyone who hangs on a tree'),"

Galatians 5:11 "And I, brethren, if I still preach circumcision, why do I still suffer persecution? Then the offense of the cross has ceased."

Colossians 2:14 "having wiped out the handwriting of requirements that was against us, which was contrary to us. And He has taken it out of the way, having nailed it to the cross."

Colossians 2:15 "Having disarmed principalities and powers, He made a public spectacle of them, triumphing over them in it."

Hebrews 8:10 "For this is the covenant that I will make with the house of Israel after those days, says the LORD: I will put My laws in their mind and write them on their hearts; and I will be their God, and they shall be My people."

Galatians 4:5 "to redeem those who were under the law, that we might receive the adoption as sons."

Blood

Matthew 26:28 "For this is My blood of the new covenant, which is shed for many for the remission of sins."

Mark 14:24 "And He said to them, "This is My blood of the new covenant, which is shed for many."

John 6:53 "Then Jesus said to them, "Most assuredly, I say to you, unless you eat the flesh of the Son of Man and drink His blood, you have no life in you."

John 6:54 "Whoever eats My flesh and drinks My blood has eternal life, and I will raise him up at the last day."

Acts 20:28 "Therefore take heed to yourselves and to all the flock, among which the Holy Spirit has made you overseers, to shepherd the church of God which He purchased with His own blood."

Ephesians 2:13 "But now in Christ Jesus you who once were far off have been brought near by the blood of Christ."

Colossians 1:20 "and by Him to reconcile all things to Himself, by Him, whether things on earth or things in heaven, having made peace through the blood of His cross."

Hebrews 9:12 "Not with the blood of goats and calves, but with His own blood He entered the Most Holy Place once for all, having obtained eternal redemption."

Hebrews 9:14 "how much more shall the blood of Christ, who through the eternal Spirit offered Himself without spot to God, cleanse your conscience from dead works to serve the living God?"

Hebrews 10:29 "Of how much worse punishment, do you suppose, will he be thought worthy who has trampled the Son of God underfoot, counted the blood of the covenant by which he was sanctified a common thing, and insulted the Spirit of grace?"

Hebrews 12:24 "to Jesus the Mediator of the new covenant, and to the blood of sprinkling that speaks better things than that of Abel."

Hebrews 13:12 "Therefore Jesus also, that He might sanctify the people with His own blood, suffered outside the gate."

Hebrews 13:20 "Now may the God of peace who brought up our Lord Jesus from the dead, that great Shepherd of the sheep, through the blood of the everlasting covenant,"

1 Peter 1:2 "elect according to the foreknowledge of God the Father, in sanctification of the Spirit, for obedience and sprinkling of the blood of Jesus Christ: Grace to you and peace be multiplied."

1 Peter 1:18-19 "knowing that you were not redeemed with corruptible things, like silver or gold, from your aimless conduct received by tradition from your fathers, but with the precious blood of Christ, as of a lamb without blemish and without spot."

1 John 1:7 "But if we walk in the light as He is in the light, we have fellowship with one another, and the blood of Jesus Christ His Son cleanses us from all sin."

1 John 1:9 "If we confess our sins, He is faithful and just to forgive us our sins and to cleanse us from all unrighteousness."

1 John 5:8 "And there are three that bear witness on earth: the Spirit, the water, and the blood; and these three agree as one."

Revelation 1:5 "and from Jesus Christ, the faithful witness, the firstborn from the dead, and the ruler over the kings of the earth. To Him who loved us and washed us from our sins in His own blood,"

Revelation 5:9-10 "And they sang a new song, saying: 'You are worthy to take the scroll, And to open its seals; For You were slain, And have redeemed us to God by Your blood Out of every tribe and tongue and people and nation, And have made us kings and priests to our God; And we shall reign on the earth.'"

Revelation 7:14 "And I said to him, 'Sir, you know.' So he said to me, 'These are the ones who come out of the great tribulation, and washed their robes and made them white in the blood of the Lamb.'"

As a pioneer, captain, or author (archegos, aitios)

Acts 3:15 "and killed the Prince of life, whom God raised from the dead, of which we are witnesses."

Acts 5:31 "Him God has exalted to His right hand to be Prince and Savior, to give repentance to Israel and forgiveness of sins."

Hebrews 2:10 "For it was fitting for Him, for whom are all things and by whom are all things, in bringing many sons to glory, to make the captain of their salvation perfect through sufferings."

Hebrews 12:2 "looking unto Jesus, the author and finisher of our faith, who for the joy that was set before Him endured the cross, despising the shame, and has sat down at the right hand of the throne of God."

Hebrews 5:9 "And having been perfected, He became the author of eternal salvation to all who obey Him,"

Resurrection

John 10:17 "Therefore My Father loves Me, because I lay down My life that I may take it again."

Acts 2:24 "whom God raised up, having loosed the pains of death, because it was not possible that He should be held by it."

Acts 4:33 "And with great power the apostles gave witness to the resurrection of the Lord Jesus. And great grace was upon them all."

Acts 13:23 "From this man's seed, according to the promise, God raised up for Israel a Savior—Jesus." (*The message is that Jesus has been raised up.*)

Acts 16:31 "So they said, 'Believe on the Lord Jesus Christ [resurrected Christ], and you will be saved, you and your household.'"

Acts 17:3 "explaining and demonstrating that the Christ had to suffer and rise again from the dead, and saying, 'This Jesus whom I preach to you is the Christ.'"

Acts 17:31 "because He has appointed a day on which He will judge the world in righteousness by the Man whom He has ordained. He has given assurance of this to all by raising Him from the dead."

Romans 1:4 "and declared to be the Son of God with power according to the Spirit of holiness, by the resurrection from the dead."

Romans 4:24 "but also for us. It shall be imputed to us who believe in Him who raised up Jesus our Lord from the dead,"

Romans 4:25 "who was delivered up because of our offenses, and was raised because of our justification."

1 Corinthians 15:17 "And if Christ is not risen, your faith is futile; you are still in your sins!"

Philippians 3:11 "if, by any means, I may attain to the resurrection from the dead."

Philippians 3:12 "Not that I have already attained, or am already perfected; but I press on, that I may lay hold of that for which Christ Jesus has also laid hold of me."

2 Timothy 2:8 "Remember that Jesus Christ, of the seed of David, was raised from the dead according to my gospel,"

Hebrews 1:5 "For to which of the angels did He ever say:
'You are My Son,
Today I have begotten You'?
    And again:
'I will be to Him a Father,
And He shall be to Me a Son'?"

Romans 8:34 "Who is he who condemns? It is Christ who died, and furthermore is also risen, who is even at the right hand of God, who also makes intercession for us."

1 Peter 1:3 "Blessed be the God and Father of our Lord Jesus Christ, who according to His abundant mercy has begotten us again to a living hope through the resurrection of Jesus Christ from the dead,"

1 Peter 3:18 "For Christ also suffered once for sins, the just for the unjust, that He might bring us to God, being put to death in the flesh but made alive by the Spirit,"

Non-specific or ambiguous

Luke 9:22 "saying, 'The Son of Man must suffer many things, and be rejected by the elders and chief priests and scribes, and be killed, and be raised the third day.'"

Luke 12:50 "But I have a baptism to be baptized with, and how distressed I am till it is accomplished!"

Luke 24:26 "Ought not the Christ to have suffered these things and to enter into His glory?"

Luke 24:44 "Then He said to them, 'These are the words which I spoke to you while I was still with you, that all things must be fulfilled which were written in the Law of Moses and the Prophets and the Psalms concerning Me.'"

Luke 24:46 "Then He said to them, 'Thus it is written, and thus it was necessary for the Christ to suffer and to rise from the dead the third day,'"

John 1:12 "But as many as received Him, to them He gave the right to become children of God, to those who believe in His name:"

John 1:17 "For the law was given through Moses, but grace and truth came through Jesus Christ."

John 1:18 "No one has seen God at any time. The only

begotten Son, who is in the bosom of the Father, He has declared Him."

John 3:14 "And as Moses lifted up the serpent in the wilderness, even so must the Son of Man be lifted up,"

John 10:15 "As the Father knows Me, even so I know the Father; and I lay down My life for the sheep."

John 11:52 "and not for that nation only, but also that He would gather together in one the children of God who were scattered abroad."

John 12:32 "And I, if I am lifted up from the earth, will draw all peoples to Myself."

Acts 26:23 "that the Christ would suffer, that He would be the first to rise from the dead, and would proclaim light to the Jewish people and to the Gentiles."

Romans 5:6 "For when we were still without strength, in due time Christ died for the ungodly."

Romans 5:8 "But God demonstrates His own love toward us, in that while we were still sinners, Christ died for us."

Romans 5:10 "For if when we were enemies we were reconciled to God through the death of His Son, much more, having been reconciled, we shall be saved by His life."

Romans 5:19 "For as by one man's disobedience many were made sinners, so also by one Man's obedience many will be made righteous."

1 Corinthians 1:18 "For the message of the cross is foolishness to those who are perishing, but to us who are being saved it is the power of God."

1 Corinthians 1:23 "but we preach Christ crucified, to the Jews a stumbling block and to the Greeks foolishness,"

1 Corinthians 2:2 "For I determined not to know anything among you except Jesus Christ and Him crucified."

1 Corinthians 8:11 "And because of your knowledge shall the weak brother perish, for whom Christ died?"

1 Corinthians 15:3 "For I delivered to you first of all that which I also received: that Christ died for our sins according to the Scriptures,"

1 Corinthians 15:57 "But thanks be to God, who gives us the victory through our Lord Jesus Christ."

Galatians 3:13 "Christ has redeemed us from the curse of the law, having become a curse for us (for it is written, 'Cursed is everyone who hangs on a tree'),"

Galatians 5:11 "And I, brethren, if I still preach circumcision, why do I still suffer persecution? Then the offense of the cross has ceased."

Ephesians 2:13 "But now in Christ Jesus you who once were far off have been brought near by the blood of Christ."

1 Thessalonians 1:10 "and to wait for His Son from heaven, whom He raised from the dead, even Jesus who delivers us from the wrath to come."

1 Thessalonians 5:9 "For God did not appoint us to wrath, but to obtain salvation through our Lord Jesus Christ,"

1 Timothy 1:15 "This is a faithful saying and worthy of all acceptance, that Christ Jesus came into the world to save sinners, of whom I am chief."

1 Timothy 3:16 "And without controversy great is the mystery of godliness:
God was manifested in the flesh,
Justified in the Spirit,
Seen by angels,
Preached among the Gentiles,
Believed on in the world,
Received up in glory."

Miscellaneous items

This shows that Jesus' death was a glorification.

John 13:31 "So, when he had gone out, Jesus said, 'Now the Son of Man is glorified, and God is glorified in Him.'"

John 13:32 "If God is glorified in Him, God will also glorify Him in Himself, and glorify Him *immediately*." (emphasis added)

Salvation

Acts 26:20 "but declared first to those in Damascus and in Jerusalem, and throughout all the region of Judea, and then to the Gentiles, that they should repent, turn to God, and do works befitting repentance."

Romans 10:9 "that if you confess with your mouth the Lord Jesus and believe in your heart that God has raised Him from the dead, you will be saved."

The Spirit does the work of Salvation

1 Corinthians 6:11 "And such were some of you. But you were washed, but you were sanctified, but you were justified in the name of the Lord Jesus and by the Spirit of our God."

1 Corinthians 12:13 "For by one Spirit we were all baptized into one body– whether Jews or Greeks, whether slaves or free-- and have all been made to drink into one Spirit."

2 Corinthians 3:17-18 "Now the Lord is the Spirit; and where the Spirit of the Lord is, there is liberty. But we all with unveiled face, beholding as in a mirror the glory of the Lord, are being transformed into the same image from glory to glory, just as by the Spirit of the Lord."

2 Thessalonians 2:13 "But we are bound to give thanks to God always for you, brethren beloved by the Lord, because God from the beginning chose you for salvation through sanctification by the Spirit and belief in the truth,"

Titus 3:5 "not by works of righteousness which we have done, but according to His mercy He saved us, through the washing of regeneration and renewing of the Holy Spirit,"

Titus 3:6 "whom He poured out on us abundantly through Jesus Christ our Savior,"

BIBLIOGRAPHY

Acts17Apologetics, "'Does God Exist?' David Wood vs. Michael Shermer (Christian vs. Atheist Debate)," Acts17Apologetics, Published on October 30, 2016, YouTube video, at 47:10.
https://www.youtube.com/watch?v=PMWKm40-dnM

Anselm, St. *The Works of St. Anselm, Cur Deus Homo,* Translated by Sidney Norton Dean, Book 1, Chap. 12, Sacred Texts, accessed October 31, 2017.
https://www.sacred-texts.com/chr/ans/ans117.htm

Aulen, Gustav. *Christus Victor,* translated by A. G. Hebert. Eugene, OR, Wipf and Stock Publishers, 2003

Bercot, David: *What the Early Christians Believed About the Atonement,* audio CD, Amberson, PA: Scroll Publishing, August 8, 2006.

Brown, Colin. *New International Dictionary of New Testament Theology, Vol. III, p. 151* s.v. "Reconciliation," Grand Rapids, MI: Zondervan, 1971.

Crider, Keith. *Sacrifice or Penalty? Why it matters what we believe about Christ's death.* Harrisonburg, VA: Christian Light Publications, 2018.

Comfort, Ray. "Are you Good Enough to go to Heaven?" Bellflower, CA: Living Waters Publications, gospel tract.

Darrell, "What Is the Eastern Orthodox View of the Atonement," Tough Questions Answered, November 9, 2011. https://www.toughquestionsanswered.org/2011/11/09/the-recapitulation-theory/

Driver, John. *Understanding the Atonement for the Mission of the Church.* Scottsdale, PA: Herald Press, 1986.

Hansen, Ethan, "My favorite verse," Mat-Su Valley Frontiersman, accessed January 19, 2020. https://www.frontiersman.com/my-favorite-bible-verse/article_b4d2fa08-b35b-11e7-9b7f-77ca0fa16040.html.

Herrman, Johannes, *Theological Dictionary of the New Testament Vol III*, s.v. "hilaskomai, hilasmos," Grand Rapids, MI: Wm. B. Eerdmans Publishing Company, 1964.

Hodge, Charles. "Justification Is a Forensic Act," A Puritan's Mind, accessed April 18, 2020. https://www.apuritansmind.com/justification/justification-is-a-forensic-act-by-dr-charles-hodge/

Jefferson, Thomas, "The Declaration of Independence", 1776

Lewis, C.S. *Mere Christianity*, New York: Harper Collins, 2001.

McDowell, Josh. *More Than a Carpenter*, Tyndale House Publishers, 2009.

McGrath, Alister E.: *Luther's Theology of the Cross: Martin Luther's Theological Breakthrough.* Oxford, UK; Malden, MA: Blackwell Publishers, 2000.

Mathis, David. "The Gospel of James: Open Letter to Martin Luther," Desiring God, accessed December 14, 2019. https://www.desiringgod.org/articles/the-gospel-of-james

Murray, Andrew. *The Blood of the Cross,* New Kensington, PA: Whittaker House, 1981.

Packer, J. I. "What did the Cross Achieve? The Logic of Penal Substitution", The Gospel Coalition, accessed April 18, 2020. https://resources.thegospelcoalition.org/library/what-did-the-cross-achieve-the-logic-of-penal-substitution

—— "Sola Fide: The Reformed Doctrine of Justification". Ligonier.org. Accessed December 13, 2019. https://www.ligonier.org/learn/articles/sola-fide-the-reformed-doctrine-of-justification/

Piper, John. *Counted Righteous in Christ,* 69. Accessed 12/13/19, https://document.desiringgod.org/counted-righteous-in-christ-en.pdf

Pulliam, Ken, "Why I De-converted from Evangelical Christianity," Former Fundy, accessed December 29, 2109. http://formerfundy.blogspot.com/2010/07/faustus-socinus-on-penal-substitution_29.html

Roper, Ronald L. "Premial Justice, the Unjust Cross, and Power from on High [Complete Paper]," The Premial Atonement: accessed November 24, 2019. https://premialatonement.wordpress.com/premial-justice-the-unjust-cross-and-power-from-on-high/

―― "Appendix: God's Premial Justice in the Psalms," The Premial Atonement, accessed November 1, 2017. https://premialatonement.wordpress.com/appendix-gods-premial-justice-in-the-psalms/

Scott, Waldron Byron. *What about the Cross: Exploring Models of the Atonement.* Lincoln, NE: iUniverse, 2007.

Seely, David Rolf. "William Tyndale and the Language of At-One-Ment," Religious Studies Center, accessed November 1, 2017. https://rsc.byu.edu/archived/king-james-bible-and-restoration/3-william-tyndale-and-language-one-ment

Schrenk, Gottlob. *Theological Dictionary of the New Testament, Vol. II.* S.v. "dikaiosyne," Grand Rapids, MI, Wm. B. Eerdmans Publishing, 1964.

Socinus, Faustus. *De Jesu Christus Servatore, Part III.* Translated by Alan Gomes.

Sproul, R. C. "Treasuring Redemption's Price", Ligonier Ministries, accessed April 20, 2020. https://www.ligonier.org/learn/devotionals/treasuring-redemptions-price/

―― *The Truth of The Cross.* Reformation Trust Publishing, 2007.

―― "The Very Heart of the Reformation." Ligonier, accessed December 13, 2019. https://www.ligonier.org/blog/very-heart-reformation/

The Skeptics Annotated Bible, "Are We Punished for the Sins

of Others?" The Skeptics Annotated Bible, accessed December 2, 2019. https://skepticsannotatedbible.com/contra/iniquity.html

Stauffer, J.L. *What Jesus Did for Us on the Cross: An Anabaptist response to popular errors about Jesus' work for us.* Harrisonburg, VA: Christian Light Publications, 2007.

Thompson, Francis. "The Veteran of Heaven," *Masterpieces of Religious Verse,* New York: Harper and Brothers Publishers, 1948.

Tozer, A. W. "Christian Quotes," oChristian, accessed November 24, 2019. http://christian-quotes.ochristian.com/Light-Quotes/page-4.shtml

Treat, Jeremy. *The Crucified King: Atonement and Kingdom in Biblical and Systematic Theology,* Grand Rapids, MI: Zondervan, 2014.

Trenham, Archpriest Josiah. *Rock and Sand: An Orthodox Appraisal of the Protestant Reformers and Their Teachings.* Columbia, MO: Newrome Press LLC, 2018.

Wesley, John *The Works of the Reverend John Wesley, A. M.* J. Emory and B. Waugh, J Collard Printer, 1831. Accessed February 5, 2020 https://archive.org/details/03553688.1116.emory.edu/page/n1/mode/2up

The Westminster Larger Catechism, A Puritan's Mind, accessed 11/28/19, http://www.apuritansmind.com/westminster-standards/larger-catechism/

Westminster Confession

White, James, and Hunt, Dave. *Debating Calvinism: Five Points, Two Views.* Colorado Springs, CO: Multmonah Books, 2004

Wright, N.T. *The Day the Revolution Began: Reconsidering the Meaning of Jesus' Crucifixion.* San Francisco: HarperOne, 2016.

Young, Ken. "Faithful Love." *Songs of Faith and Praise,* West Monroe, LA: Howard Publishing, 1994.